The Sandusky Tool Company

ESTABLISHED 1868

SANDUSKY, OHIO, U.S.A.

CATALOG No. 25

SEPTEMBER 1st, 1925

THE ASTRAGAL PRESS
Mendham, New Jersey

Library of Congress Catalogue Card Number:
91-78044
International Standard Book Number:
978-1-879335-26-4

Published by
The Astragal Press
P.O. Box 239
Mendham, New Jersey 07945-0239

The Sandusky Tool Company

ESTABLISHED 1868

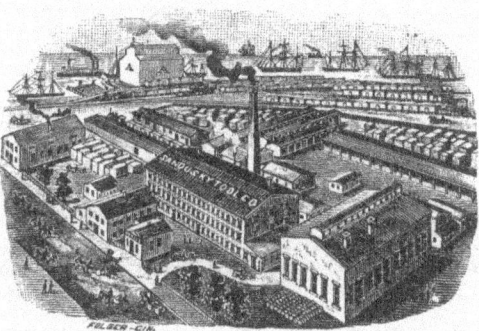

GEORGE A. SCHWER,
President

WILLIAM F. SEITZ,
Vice-President

WILBERT G. SCHWER,
Secretary

ALDEN SEITZ,
Treasurer

SANDUSKY, OHIO, SEPT. 1, 1925.

To Our Customers:

We take pleasure in submitting for your examination our new catalog No. 25.

This catalog cancels all previously issued catalogs and bulletins, and we urge our customers to destroy all such printed matter and to order only from this catalog.

In addition to all of the well-known products we have been manufacturing for nearly sixty years, this catalog illustrates and describes many new products which we confidently expect will be of great interest to our customers.

We wish to emphasize the fact that our policies are progressive in every respect. We believe that we have brought our line of products thoroughly up-to-date with the additions shown in this catalog, and it will be our endeavor to keep abreast of the times by adding more and more lines every year.

We are prepared to quote attractive prices on special work of all kinds, and we earnestly solicit inquiries from our customers who are in the market for tools or hardware of any kind. Our plant presents a combination which is extremely unique, as we have a sawmill, woodworking shop, machine shop, forge shop, and a rolling and stamping mill, all under one roof. We are, consequently, well equipped for manufacturing a vast number of articles, and are always ready to place our facilities at the disposal of our customers.

All of our products are fully warranted as regards workmanship and materials, and we endeavor to give the best of service at all times.

Yours very truly,

THE SANDUSKY TOOL COMPANY.

Geo. A. Schwer

President.

SANDUSKY SEMI-STEEL AND ADJUSTABLE WOOD BENCH PLANES

Note from the Publisher: - The Semi-Steel used for the body of the plane was a special alloy composed of 85% gray iron, 10% steel and 5% Mayari iron.(probably a Cuban ore) The patent application for this plane was filed by Wilbert G. Schwer on October 14,1925 and granted to him on December 28, 1928, (U.S. Patent #1,696,584) which was assigned to Sandusky Tool Corporation.

"Sandusky" Semi-Steel Bench Planes

These planes are the simplest and most mechanically perfect metal planes on the market. They have considerably fewer parts than any other plane, and at the same time have every adjustment feature possessed by other types.

Having considerably fewer parts than the ordinary iron plane, the "Sandusky" Semi-Steel Plane is lighter in weight, and is consequently less fatiguing when used for long periods at a time. Furthermore, the parts eliminated by this improved adjusting mechanism are the very parts which are most easily broken in the ordinary iron plane. With reasonably good care, the "Sandusky" Plane will last indefinitely.

The "Sandusky" Semi-Steel Plane is equipped with our famous heavy plane iron or cutter, identical in quality with those we have used in all our planes, both wood and metal, for nearly sixty years. The cutter will, therefore, take and retain a much finer cutting edge than a thin cutter, and will wear indefinitely. It cannot possibly spring or chatter when used against hard woods.

The cap is so constructed as to make the cutter a double iron, and the distance of the cap from the cutting edge is automatically adjusted by regulating the depth of the cut in the manner described below.

The retaining nut, located above the cutter, when turned tightly to the right, holds the cutter so rigidly that the plane may be used against the hardest woods for hours at a time without disturbing the adjustment or the depth of the cut in the slightest degree.

The cut of the iron is regulated by merely loosening the retaining nut by turning it one complete revolution to the left, and then raising or lowering the iron or cutter to the desired position by turning the adjusting nut one way or the other. When the correct depth is obtained, the cutter may be squared up with the bottom of the plane by moving the side adjusting lever to one side or the other, and then locked firmly into position by turning the retaining nut to the right.

The body of the "Sandusky" Plane is made of fine-textured semi-steel, brightly polished on the sides and bottom, and with the upper portion painted with dark blue enamel. The handles and knobs are made of carefully-selected hardwood, stained and varnished to blend attractively with the rest of the plane.

"Sandusky" Semi-Steel Bench Planes
Patent Pending

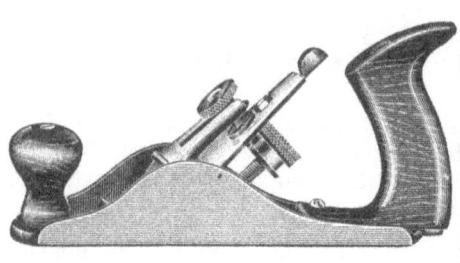

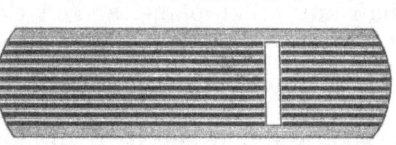

Smooth Bottom

Corrugated Bottom

Nos. 3S and 3SC

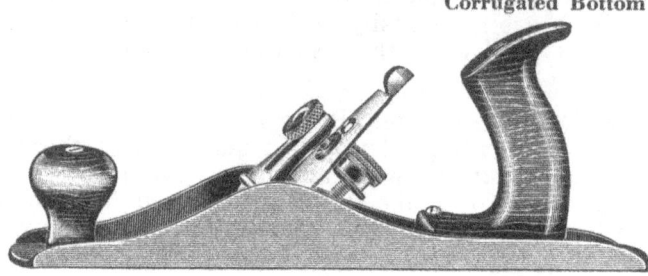

Nos. 13S and 13SC

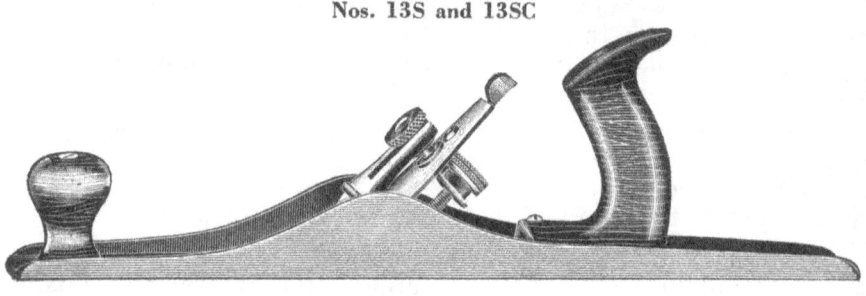

Nos. 19S and 19SC

Stock No.:		Price Each:
3 S	Semi-Steel Smoothing Plane, 9″ Long, 2″ Double Iron, with Smooth Bottom; Weight, 2¾ lbs.	$ 5.00
13 S	Semi-Steel Jack Plane, 14″ Long, 2″ Double Iron, with Smooth Bottom; Weight, 4 lbs.	5.65
19 S	Semi-Steel Fore Plane, 18″ Long, 2¼″ Double Iron, with Smooth Bottom; Weight, 6 lbs.	7.25
3 SC	Semi-Steel Smoothing Plane, 9″ Long, 2″ Double Iron, with Corrugated Bottom; Weight, 2¾ lbs.	5.00
13 SC	Semi-Steel Jack Plane, 14″ Long, 2″ Double Iron, with Corrugated Bottom; Weight, 4 lbs.	5.65
19 SC	Semi-Steel Fore Plane, 18″ Long, 2¼″ Double Iron, with Corrugated Bottom; Weight, 6 lbs.	7.25

Packed One Plane in a Labeled Cardboard Box; twelve planes in a case.

Semi-Steel Block Planes

Stock No.:		Price Each:
2 S	Semi-Steel Block Plane, 6½″ Long, 1-5/8″ Iron, with Nickel-Plated Cap and Smooth Bottom; Weight, 1½ lbs.	$ 2.50

"Sandusky" Adjustable Wood Bench Planes

These are our standard wood planes equipped with the same adjusting mechanism as our semi-steel planes, and consequently having all the advantages of both.

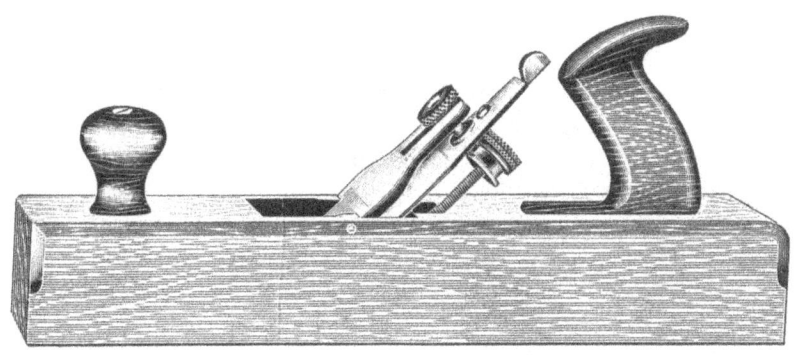

Stock No:		Price Each:
5½W	"Sandusky" Adjustable Wood Smoothing Plane, 10⅝″ Long, with Jack Handle and 2¼″ Double Iron	$5.00
13W	"Sandusky" Adjustable Wood Jack Plane, 16″ Long, with 2¼″ Double Iron	5.00
19W	"Sandusky" Adjustable Wood Fore Plane, 22″ Long, with 2¼″ Double Iron	6.25

Extra Caps for Adjustable Wood Planes	$1.00
Extra Irons, or Cutters, for Adjustable Wood Planes	1.75

(For prices of the other parts of the adjusting mechanism, see list on page eight.)

The following parts drawing illustrates the greatly simplified and improved mechanism of the "Sandusky" Semi-Steel Bench Planes:

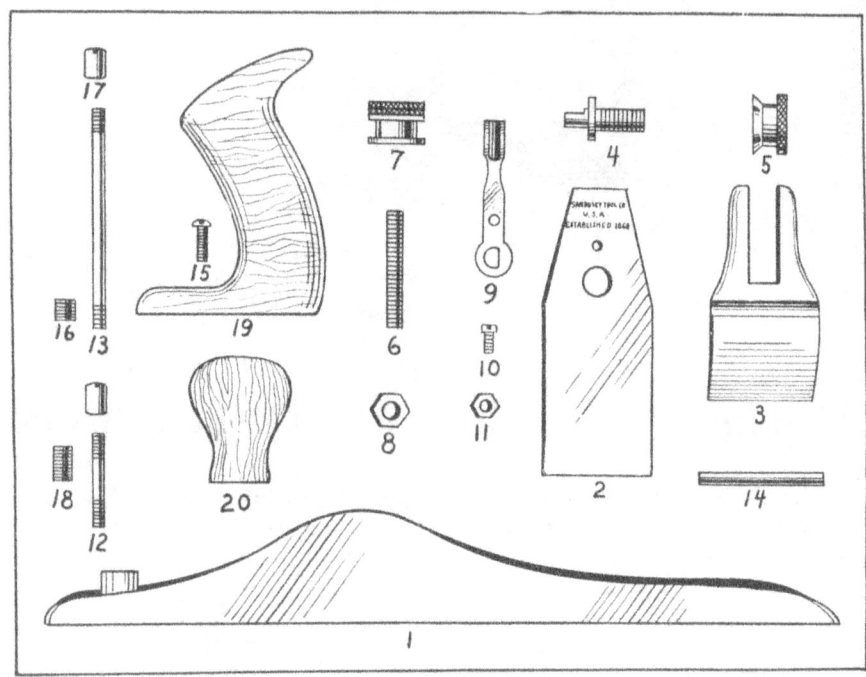

Price List of Extra Parts for "Sandusky" Semi-Steel Bench Planes

Part No:		Price Each:
1	Plane Body	
	For Smoothing Plane	1.25
	For Jack Plane	2.00
	For Fore Plane	4.75
2	Plane Iron, or Cutter	
	For Smoothing or Jack Plane	1.50
	For Fore Plane	1.50
3	Plane Iron Cap	
	For Smoothing or Jack Plane	.60
	For Fore Plane	.60
4	Retaining Stud	.50
5	Retaining Nut	.60
6	Regulating Stud	.25
7	Regulating Nut	.60
8	Regulating Stud Lock Nut	.10
9	Side Adjusting Lever	.25
10	Side Adjusting Lever Screw	.15
11	Side Adjusting Lever Screw Lock Nut	.10
12	Knob Stud	.15
13	Handle Stud	.15
14	Fulcrum Pin	
	For Smoothing or Jack Plane	.15
	For Fore Plane	.20
15	Handle Screw	.10
16	Handle Boss Bushing	.10
17	Knob or Handle Nut	.15
18	Knob Boss Bushing	.10
19	Handle	.60
20	Knob	.30

With the exception of Nos. 1, 2, 3, and 14, the parts of all three sizes of bench planes are interchangeable. Parts 4, 5, 7, 8, 9, 10, 11, and 20 fit any of the Adjustable Wood Planes.

HOES

AND

FORGED

PRODUCTS

Note from the Publisher: - "SCHWEHR'S IMPROVED
GERMAN HOE" was developed by Albert Schwer in the
early 1870's. Forged from a single piece of steel,
Sandusky Tool Co. was the sole manufacturer for
this design of hoe and obtained patents on the
machinery used. This hoe is noted in the *1877 Catalog*.
It was likely the line of hoes and forged garden
tools that encouraged the American Fork and Hoe Co.,
(now True Temper, Inc.) to purchase Sandusky Tool
Company on March 1, 1926.

Eye Hoes

We are the originators of eye hoes with the eye and blade forged from a single piece of high-carbon spring steel, and for many years were the sole manufacturers. Our eye hoes are made by our special process, covered by U. S. Patent No. 216,224, of June 3rd, 1879.

"Sandusky" Spring-Steel Hoes will take and retain a very sharp cutting edge, and will not wear out in sandy or gravelly soils. They are so strong as to be practically indestructable, and will give years of service.

Planter's Pattern Hoes

Planter's Pattern

This is our best-selling hoe in export markets, and is also very popular throughout the southern states.

German Pattern Square-Eye Hoes, when sold without handles, have the same prices as the Planter's Pattern.

The following prices are for half-polished hoes in natural oil-finish. For full-polished hoes, add fifty cents per dozen.

PRICE LIST

Nos	4/0	3/0	2/0	1/0	1	2	3	4	5	6
Width of Blade	5½"	6"	6½"	7"	7½"	8"	8½"	9"	9½"	10"
Price per Doz	$5.50	$5.50	$5.50	$5.75	$6.00	$6.50	$7.00	$7.50	$8.00	$8.50

Scovil Pattern Hoes and Lyndon Pattern Hoes

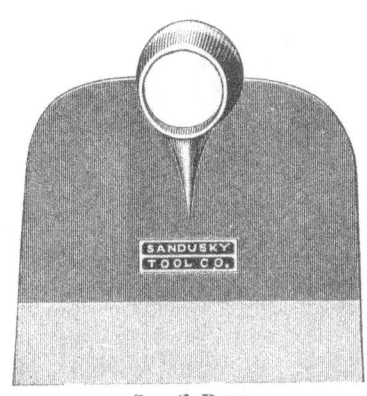
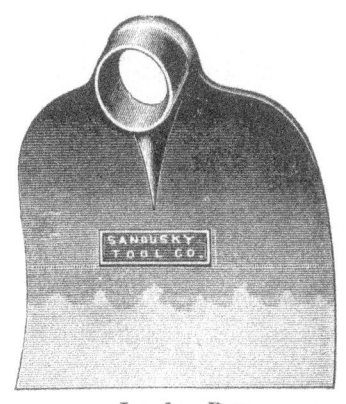

Scovil Pattern   Lyndon Pattern

The Scovil Pattern Hoe is extremely popular in both the domestic and the foreign markets, and is probably the best eye hoe for general use.

The Lyndon Pattern Hoe differs from the Scovil only in that the blade of the former is "set", or curved, instead of being straight.

PRICE LIST
SCOVIL AND LYNDON PATTERN HOES

Nos	4/0	3/0	2/0	1/0	1	2	3	4	5	6
Width of Blade	5½"	6"	6½"	7"	7½"	8"	8½"	9"	9½"	10"
Price per Doz	$5.75	$5.75	$5.75	$6.00	$6.25	$6.75	$7.25	$7.75	$8.25	$8.75

Oval-Eye Grub or Sprouting Hoes

German Pattern Square-Eye Grub Hoes, when sold without handles, have the same prices as Oval-Eye Grub Hoes.

The following prices are for half-polished hoes in natural oil-finish. For full-polished hoes, add fifty cents per dozen.

PRICE LIST

Nos	7/0	6/0	5/0	4/0
Width of Blade	4"	4½"	5"	5½"
Price per Doz	$6.50	$7.00	$7.50	$8.00

Rice or Cane Hoes and Hilling Hoes

Rice Hoe

Hilling Hoe

The following prices are for half-polished hoes in natural oil-finish. For full-polished hoes, add fifty cents per dozen.

PRICE LIST—Rice or Cane Hoes

Nos	5/0	4/0	3/0	2/0	1/0
Size of Blade	5"x7½"	5½"x7¾"	6"x8"	6½"x8¼"	7"x8½"
Price per Doz	$6.50	$7.00	$7.50	$8.00	$8.50

PRICE LIST—Hilling Hoes

Nos	7/0	6/0	5/0	4/0	3/0	2/0	1/0
Width of Blade	4"	4½"	5"	5½"	6"	6½"	7"
Price per Doz	$5.00	$5.00	$5.00	$5.50	$6.00	$6.50	$7.00

Giant Pattern Hoes — Full-Polished

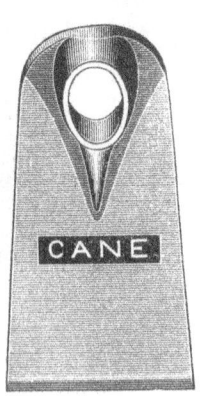

PRICE LIST

Sprouting Hoes, Size 4" x 9" .... $7.50 Per Dozen
Hilling Hoes, Size 6" x 8" .... 7.50 Per Dozen
Cane Hoes, Size 4½" x 8" .... 7.50 Per Dozen

Giant Planter's Hoes

Nos	3/0	2/0	1/0	1	2
Width of Blade	6"	6½"	7"	7½"	8"
Price per Doz	$6.00	$6.25	$6.50	$6.75	$7.00

Notice

When shipped without handles, eye hoes are usually packed in barrels containing twenty-five to thirty dozen hoes each, depending on the size of the hoes. Consequently, many customers find it convenient to order eye hoes in terms of "barrels", which we always understand to mean approximately twenty-five to thirty dozen.

A barrel of average-sized hoes weighs about 550 pounds.

Handled hoes are shipped in bundles of one dozen, with the blades covered with oiled paper and strong burlap.

A bundle of one dozen handled hoes weighs about 45 to 50 pounds.

German Pattern Handled Square-Eye Hoes

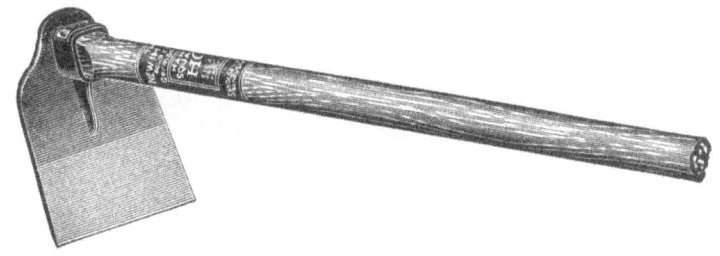

We are the originators of these internationally-famous hoes, and for many years were the sole manufacturers.

The advantage of the square-eye over the round or oval-eye lies in the fact that the handle will not turn in a square-eye hoe, and is held much more rigidly.

These hoes are furnished with heavy, first-quality, 56-inch, white-ash handles, all highly polished and waxed, and with bright, attractive labels.

When sold without handles, German Pattern Square-Eye Hoes have the same prices as Planter's Pattern Hoes.

These are exceptionally strong and durable hoes, and are suitable for almost any purpose.

The following prices are for half-polished hoes in natural oil-finish. For full-polished hoes, add fifty cents per dozen.

PRICE LIST

Nos.	4/0	3/0	2/0	1/0	1	2	3	4
Width of Blade	5½"	6"	6½"	7"	7½"	8"	8½"	9"
Price per Doz.	$8.50	$9.00	$9.50	$10.00	$10.75	$11.50	$12.25	$13.00

German Pattern Handled Tobacco Hoes

These Tobacco Hoes are very similar to the regular German Pattern Handled Square-Eye Hoes in appearance, and have the same sizes and prices. They are especially adapted to the requirements of the southern tobacco plantations.

German Pattern Handled Square-Eye Grub or Sprouting Hoes

These hoes are furnished with heavy, first-quality, 4-ft., white-ash handles, all highly polished and waxed, and with bright, attractive labels.

When sold without handles, German Pattern Square-Eye Grub Hoes have the same prices as Oval-Eye Grub Hoes.

The following prices are for half-polished hoes in natural oil-finish. For full-polished hoes, add fifty cents per dozen.

PRICE LIST

Nos	7/0	6/0	5/0	4/0
Width of Blade	4″	4½″	5″	5½″
Price per Doz	$9.00	$9.50	$10.00	$10.50

Handled Heart-Shaped Square-Eye Hoes

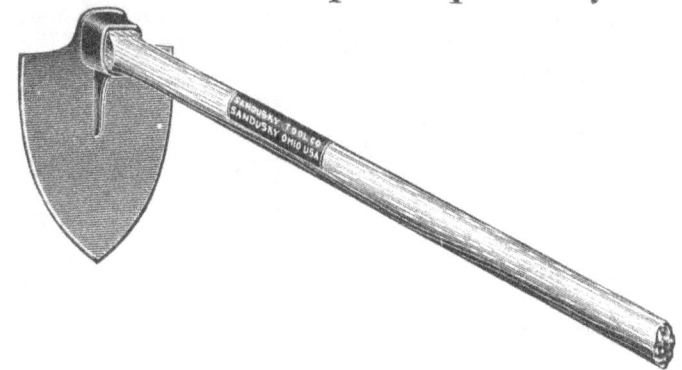

These hoes are designed for use in very hard soils, as the point and wedge-shaped blade are much easier to drive into the ground than a straight-edged hoe.

These hoes are furnished with heavy, first-quality, 4-ft., white-ash handles, all highly polished and waxed.

The following prices are for hoes in natural oil-finish.

PRICE LIST

Nos	3/0	1/0	2	4	6
Width of Blade	6″	7″	8″	9″	10″
Price per Doz	$10.20	$11.20	$12.20	$13.20	$14.20

Handled Onion or Garden Hoes

These hoes are especially adapted for use in cultivating onions, and for ordinary garden use.

The handle is 4 ft. long, and the blade 7½″ long by 3″ wide.

The following price is for half-polished hoes in natural oil-finish.

Price per Dozen, $6.90

Handled Square-Eye Grape Hoes

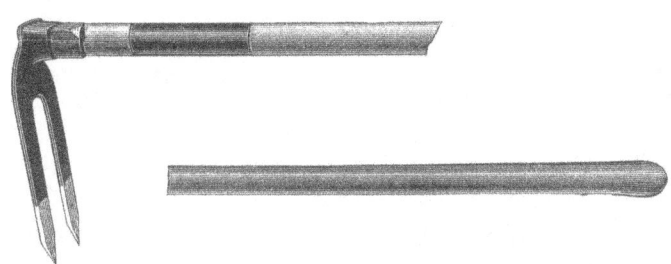

Although these hoes are primarily intended for use in vineyards, they are extensively used for cultivating gardens and for many other purposes.

Price per Dozen, $15.00

Corn Hoes

These hoes are used instead of corn knives for cutting corn.

The handle is thirty inches long, and the blade 5½″ long, 6″ wide, and 4½″ deep from the shoulder.

The following price is for half-polished hoes in natural oil-finish.

Price per Dozen, $6.50

Street Cleaning Hoes

The handle is five feet long, and the blade 6½″ deep and 14″ wide.

Price per Dozen, $15.00

"HERCULES" HANDLED HOES

Our popular "Hercules" Hoes are now available in the goose-neck pattern as well as in the familiar straight-shank design.

The shank and blade of every "Hercules" Hoe is forged from a single piece of high-carbon spring steel, which makes a much stronger hoe than if the shank were merely welded to the blade. "Hercules" Hoes are fully as strong as any of our eye hoes.

These hoes are furnished with heavy, first-quality, white-ash handles, all highly polished and waxed. The prices shown below are for 5-ft. handles, but we are prepared to furnish these hoes with 4½-ft. handles of equal quality for forty cents less per dozen.

Except for the "Hercules" Meadow Hoes, which are full-polished, the following prices are for hoes with one-third polished blades. Full-polished hoes may be had for forty cents per dozen additional.

Unless otherwise ordered, all one-third polished "Hercules" Hoes will be furnished with blades in natural oil-finish.

All types of "Hercules" Hoes have bright, attractive labels, printed in four colors.

"Hercules" Cotton or Field Hoes

"Hercules" Cotton or Field Hoes are made in three styles, as shown in the following illustrations: Straight-Shank and Curved Blade; Straight Shank and Straight Blade; and Goose-Neck Shank and Straight Blade. All three types have the same prices.

"Hercules" Cotton Scraping Hoes are sold at the same prices as "Hercules" Cotton or Field Hoes.

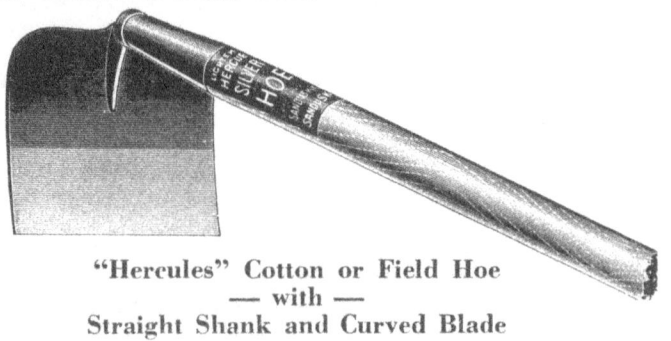

"Hercules" Cotton or Field Hoe
— with —
Straight Shank and Curved Blade

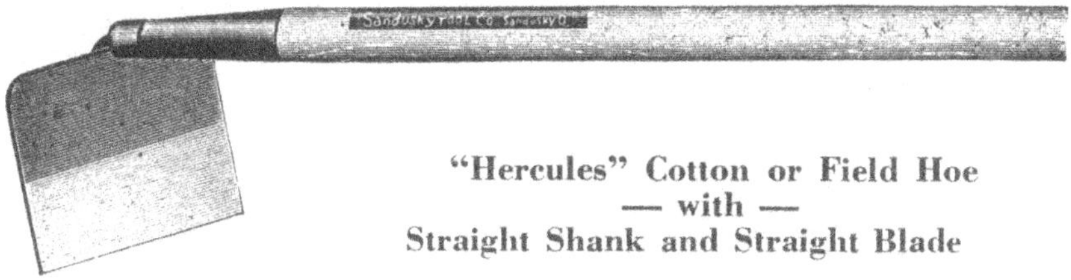

"Hercules" Cotton or Field Hoe
— with —
Straight Shank and Straight Blade

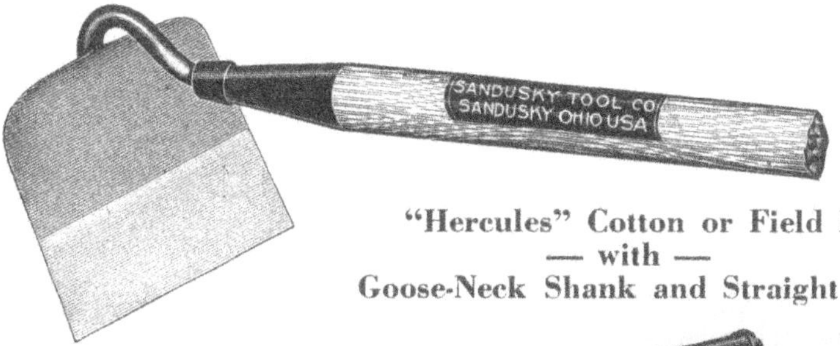

"Hercules" Cotton or Field Hoe
— with —
Goose-Neck Shank and Straight Blade

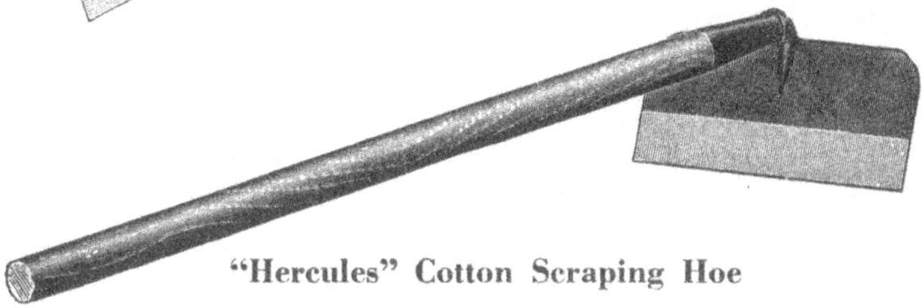

"Hercules" Cotton Scraping Hoe

PRICE LIST

Nos	3/0	2/0	1/0	1	2	3	4	5	6
Width of Blade	6"	6½"	7"	7½"	8"	8½"	9"	9½"	10"
Price per Doz	$9.60	$10.00	$10.40	$10.80	$11.20	$11.60	$12.00	$12.40	$12.80

"Hercules" Meadow Hoes

This is one of our most popular hoes, and is extensively used throughout the South.

The prices shown below are for full-polished hoes, with heavy, 5-ft., white-ash handles, all highly polished and waxed, and with bright labels.

PRICE LIST

Nos	1	2	3	4	5	6
Width of Blade	7½"	8"	8½"	9"	9½"	10"
Price per Doz	$10.20	$10.60	$11.00	$11.40	$11.80	$12.20

"Hercules" Regular Goose-Neck Hoes

Our "Hercules" Regular Goose-Neck Hoes are made in the style known as the "English Trim", and are adapted for general use in the garden and field.

These hoes are furnished with extra-quality, highly-polished, 4½-ft., white-ash handles, with bright labels. The ferrules, caps, and "goose-necks" are painted with gold enamel, making these hoes extremely attractive.

The following prices are for one-third polished hoes in natural oil-finish. For full-polished hoes, add forty cents per dozen.

PRICE LIST

Nos	3/0	1/0	2
Width of Blade	6"	7"	8"
Price per Doz	$10.40	$10.60	$10.80

Ehrhardt's Garden Hoes

These hoes are now furnished with full-sized, 4½-ft., white-ash handles, of the same quality as those supplied with our "Hercules" Hoes.

The following prices are for one-third polished hoes in natural oil-finish. For full-polished hoes, add forty cents per dozen.

PRICE LIST

Nos	3/0	2/0	1/0	1	2	3	4	5	6
Width of Blade	6"	6½"	7"	7½"	8"	8½"	9"	9½"	10"
Price per Doz	$9.20	$9.60	$10.00	$10.40	$10.80	$11.20	$11.60	$12.00	$12.40

Sidewalk Cleaners

These tools may be used for a number of purposes besides cleaning sidewalks. They make excellent scrapers for removing oil and grease from factory floors, and can be used for spading gardens and as turf edgers.

The shank and blade of our sidewalk cleaner are forged from a single piece of high-carbon spring steel, and consequently the tool is extremely strong, and will take and retain a very sharp cutting edge.

The ferrules, caps, and unpolished portions of the blades are gold-enameled; the handles are of highly-polished and waxed white ash; and the labels are printed in four colors, making these cleaners extremely attractive.

PRICE LIST

Nos	1	2	3	4
Width of Blade	7½″	8″	8½″	9″
Price per Doz	$10.00	$10.40	$10.80	$11.20

"Two-Way" Garden Hoes

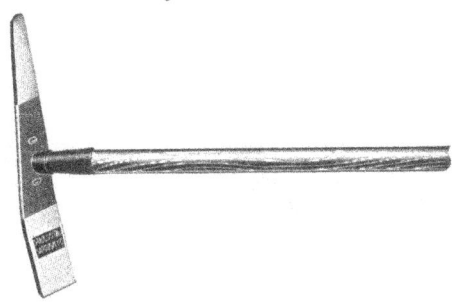

The small end of the "Two-Way" Hoe is used for hoeing between plants, and in other places where the space is too limited to permit the use of a regular-sized hoe. The large end is used as an ordinary garden hoe.

The dimensions of the blade are 1⅛″ x 3½″ x 12¼″. The handles are 4½ ft. long, with a diameter of 1″.

Although this is the lowest-priced handled hoe we manufacture, it is made from the same high-grade spring steel as all of our other hoes. Price per Dozen, $6.00

Mortar Hoes

We can convert any of our handled hoes into Mortar Hoes by merely cutting two circular holes in the blades.

The types which are most generally selected for this purpose are the No. 2 "Hercules" Regular Goose-Neck Hoe; the larger-sized "Hercules" Cotton or Field Hoes, with Straight Shanks and Straight Blades; and the Street Cleaning Hoe.

A nominal charge of forty cents additional per dozen is made for cutting the holes.

Machetes

Our machetes are forged from spring steel of very high carbon content and are consequently very durable. They are extensively used in clearing the underbrush from forests, for cutting sugar cane in Central America and the West Indies, and as corn knives in this country.

PRICE LIST

22″ Blade	**$11.00** per Dozen
24″ Blade	**13.00** per Dozen

Ice Cleavers

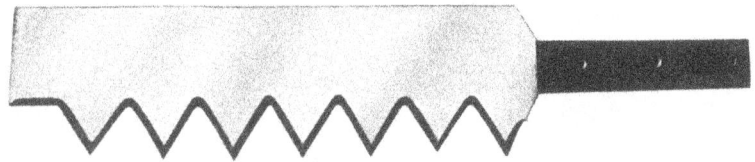

Our Ice Cleavers are made of the same quality of high-carbon spring steel as our hoes, and are very serviceable.

The Cleaver is 25″ long over all, 5⅛″ wide, with teeth 1¾″ deep. The handle is made of polished applewood, and is 7″ long and 1¾″ wide.

Price Each $4.25

WOOD TOOLS

WOOD PLANES

and

PLANE IRONS

Note from the Publisher: - Probably this was the
last published catalog of wooden planes made in
the United States. The demise of the wooden plane
is discussed in detail in *Wooden Planes in 19th
Century America*, also offered by this Publisher.
The resulting sales after publication of this
Catalog in 1925 were so discouraging to the
Management that the firm was sold in 1926, the
manufacture of these products soon after discon-
tinued, and the buildings razed in 1931.

"Sandusky" Plane Irons

Our Plane Irons or Cutters have been acknowledged to be the finest on the market for nearly sixty years.

These Irons are of the thick, wedge-shaped type familiar to all woodworkers. The cutting edges are made from a special grade of cast or tool steel laid into a soft steel backing. The Irons are beveled and ground on wet grindstones of very large diameter, which produces straight bevels and fine cutting edges, and eliminates the danger of hollow-grinding the Irons or of drawing the temper by overheating. The Irons will not retain sharp cutting edges if they are hollow-ground on wheels of small diamter, or if the temper is drawn from the steel in grinding, and if they are ruined in this way we regret that we cannot replace them.

A bevel of about twenty-five degrees will give the best results.

Bench Plane Irons

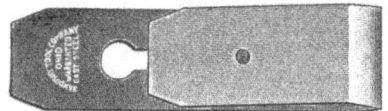

Double Iron

Single Iron

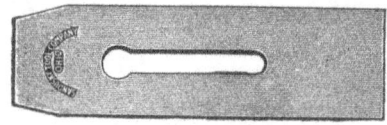

Cut Iron

Double Irons

	1½"	1⅝"	1¾"	1⅞"	2"	2⅛"
Per Dozen	$11.00	$12.00	$12.00	$12.50	$12.90	$13.20
	2¼"	2⅜"	2½"	2⅝"	2¾"	3"
Per Dozen	$14.00	$14.80	$16.40	$18.00	$20.30	$23.40

Single Irons and Cut Irons Without Caps

	1½"	1⅝"	1¾"	1⅞"	2"	2⅛"
Per Dozen	$8.00	$9.00	$9.00	$9.50	$9.90	$10.30
	2¼"	2⅜"	2½"	2⅝"	2¾"	3"
Per Dozen	$11.00	$11.80	$12.70	$14.30	$16.60	$19.70

Plane Iron Caps

	1½"	1⅝"	1¾"	1⅞"	2"	2⅛"
Per Dozen	$3.60	$3.60	$3.60	$3.60	$3.60	$3.60
	2¼"	2⅜"	2½"	2⅝"	2¾"	3"
Per Dozen	$3.60	$3.60	$4.80	$4.80	$4.80	$4.80

Soft Plane Irons (Single or Cut)

	2"	2⅛"	2¼"	2⅜"	2½"	2⅝"
Per Dozen	$9.30	$9.60	$10.30	$11.10	$11.90	$13.50
	2¾"	3"	3¼"	3½"	3¾"	4"
Per Dozen	$15.80	$18.90	$19.40	$20.30	$20.90	$21.60

Tooth Plane Irons

	$1\frac{7}{8}''$	$2''$	$2\frac{1}{8}''$	$2\frac{1}{4}''$
Per Dozen...	$12.00	$12.50	$13.00	$13.50

Soft Moulding Irons

	$\frac{1}{4}''$	$\frac{3}{8}''$	$\frac{1}{2}''$	$\frac{5}{8}''$	$\frac{3}{4}''$	$\frac{7}{8}''$
Per Dozen..............	$1.80	$1.80	$1.80	$3.90	$3.90	$3.90
	$1''$	$1\frac{1}{8}''$	$1\frac{1}{4}''$	$1\frac{3}{8}''$	$1\frac{1}{2}''$	$1\frac{5}{8}''$
Per Dozen..............	$2.00	$2.20	$2.30	$2.40	$2.50	$2.70
	$1\frac{3}{4}''$ $1\frac{7}{8}''$	$2''$	$2\frac{1}{8}''$	$2\frac{1}{4}''$	$2\frac{3}{8}''$	$2\frac{1}{2}''$
Per Dozen...... $2.90	$3.20	$3.40	$3.70	$3.90	$4.20	$4.50

Finished Moulding Irons

Finished Irons for moulding and fancy planes, one-third the prices of the complete planes.

Match Plane Irons

	$\frac{3}{8}''$	$\frac{1}{2}''$	$\frac{5}{8}''$	$\frac{3}{4}''$	$\frac{7}{8}''$	$1''$
Per Dozen..............	$4.20	$4.20	$4.20	$4.40	$4.50	$4.70

Match Plane Grooving Bits

Match Plane Grooving Bits, sizes, $\frac{1}{8}''$, 3/16", $\frac{1}{4}''$, 5/16" $7.20 per Doz.

Plank Match Plane Irons

Match Plane Irons for Plank Match Planes, size $1\frac{3}{4}''$ $7.20 per Doz.

Plank Match Plane Grooving Bits

Panel Plow Bits

Panel Plow Bits, per set of eight, sizes $\frac{1}{8}''$ to $\frac{5}{8}''$ .... $7.20 per Doz.

Filletster Plane Irons

Filletster Plane Irons, $1\frac{1}{2}''$ .... $3.84 per Doz.

Dado Plane Irons

	$\frac{3}{16}''$	$\frac{1}{4}''$	$\frac{5}{16}''$	$\frac{3}{8}''$	$\frac{1}{2}''$	$\frac{5}{8}''$	$\frac{3}{4}''$	$\frac{7}{8}''$	$1''$
Per Dozen....$2.40	$2.64	$2.88	$3.12	$3.36	$3.60	$3.84	$4.08	$4.32

Dado Plane Cutters

	$\frac{3}{16}''$	$\frac{1}{4}''$	$\frac{5}{16}''$	$\frac{3}{8}''$	$\frac{1}{2}''$	$\frac{5}{8}''$	$\frac{3}{4}''$	$\frac{7}{8}''$	$1''$
Per Dozen....$2.88	$3.12	$3.36	$3.60	$3.84	$4.08	$4.32	$4.56	$4.80

Filletster Plane Cutters

Filletster Plane Cutters .... $2.40 per Doz.

Rabbet Plane Cutters

Rabbet Plane Cutters .... $2.40 per Doz.

Irons For Coopers' Tools

Coopers' Jointer Irons

Same prices as Bench Plane Irons.

Coopers' Leveler Irons

Coopers' Leveler Irons .... $10.30 per Doz.

Coopers' Float Irons

Coopers' Float Irons, 4"-4½" wide, 7"-7½" long .... $21.60 per Doz.

Beer and Stock Howel Irons

	1¾"	2"	2⅛"	2¼"	2½"
Per Dozen........................	$9.00	$9.90	$10.30	$11.00	$12.70

Gouge Howel Irons

Gouge Howel Irons, Size 1½"....................................	$12.00 Per Dozen
V-Croze Irons for Flour Barrels.................................	7.20 Per Dozen
Plate and Thumbscrews for Lance Croze.......................	4.80 Per Dozen
Lance Croze Teeth and Hooks, Sets............................	7.20 Per Dozen
Beer Croze Teeth, Sets.......................................	12.00 Per Dozen

Special machine knives made to order from samples, patterns, or drawings. All machine knives, plane irons, etc., fully guaranteed as to materials and workmanship.

Iron Bench Screws

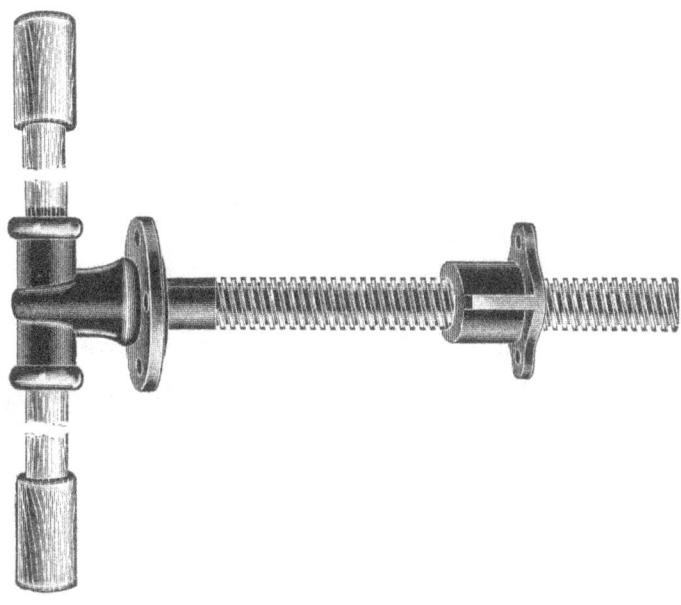

Stock No.   Price per Doz:

309   Iron Bench Screw, with Moveable Collar, Double Thread, Wrought Steel Screws, and Wood Hanle, Size, 1"x16" $14.40

"Sandusky" Self Aligning, Steel-Spindle Hand Screws

With Double-Acting Thread

The spindles of these hand screws are threaded into free-turning pivots, making it possible to adjust the jaws either parallel, as is the case with our wood hand screws, or at an angle.

The thread is reversed at the meeting point of the jaws, which causes the jaws to open or close twice as fast, when the spindles are turned, as they would if the thread ran in one direction only.

The jaws are made of selected, air-seasoned Ohio Hard Maple, and the screws of high-grade steel screw stock.

Stock No:	Length of Jaw:	Clamp Opens:	Price per doz:
708	14″	10″	$24.00
710	12″	8½″	21.60
712	10″	6″	19.20

Wood Hand Screws

The jaws of our wood hand screws are made from carefully-selected, air-seasoned, Ohio hard maple, and the screws or spindles of best second-growth hickory.

For hand screws with jaws of finest-quality American White Oak, add ten percent. to the prices shown below.

Replacement jaws or spindles for wood hand screws can only be secured from the original manufacturer, as there is no standard thread common to all makes of hand screws. The price of a single extra jaw or spindle is one-third the cost of the complete hand screw, and the price of a pair of jaws or spindles is two-thirds the cost of the complete hand screw.

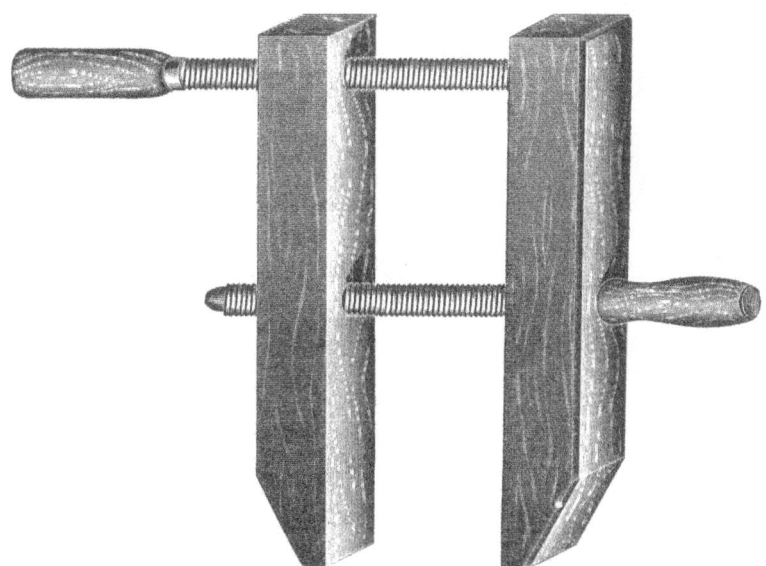

Present Stock No.	Old Stock No.	Diameter of Screw	Length of Screw	Length of Jaw	Size of Jaw	Clamp Opens	Price per Dozen
800	216¼	1¼″	28″	24″	3″ x3 ″	17″	$36.00
801	216½	1¼″	26″	22″	2¾″x2¾″	15½″	31.50
802	217	1¼″	24″	20″	2⅝″x2⅝″	13¾″	28.80
803	217¼	1¼″	22″	20″	2½″x2½″	12″	27.00
804	217½	1⅛″	22″	18″	2½″x2½″	12¼″	22.80
805	218	1⅛″	20″	18″	2⅜″x2⅜″	10½″	21.60
806	218½	1″	20″	16″	2⅜″x2⅜″	11″	20.00
807	219	1″	18″	16″	2¼″x2¼″	9¼″	18.80
808	220	⅞″	18″	14″	2⅛″x2⅛″	10″	17.60
809	221	⅞″	16″	14″	2″ x2″	8¼″	12.00
810	221½	⅞″	16″	12″	1⅞″x1⅞″	8½″	11.10
811	222	¾″	14″	12″	1¾″x1¾″	7¼″	10.20
812	223	¾″	12″	10″	1⅝″x1⅝″	5½″	8.70
813	224	⅝″	10″	8″	1⅜″x1⅜″	4½″	7.20
814	224½	⅝″	8″	7″	1⅛″x1⅛″	3″	5.70
815	225	½″	6″	5″	1″ x1″	2″	4.80
816	226	½″	5″	4″	⅞″x ⅞″	1¼″	4.20

Nos. 800-809, inclusive, packed one dozen in a case.

Nos. 810-816, inclusive, packed two dozen in a case.

Wood Bench Screws

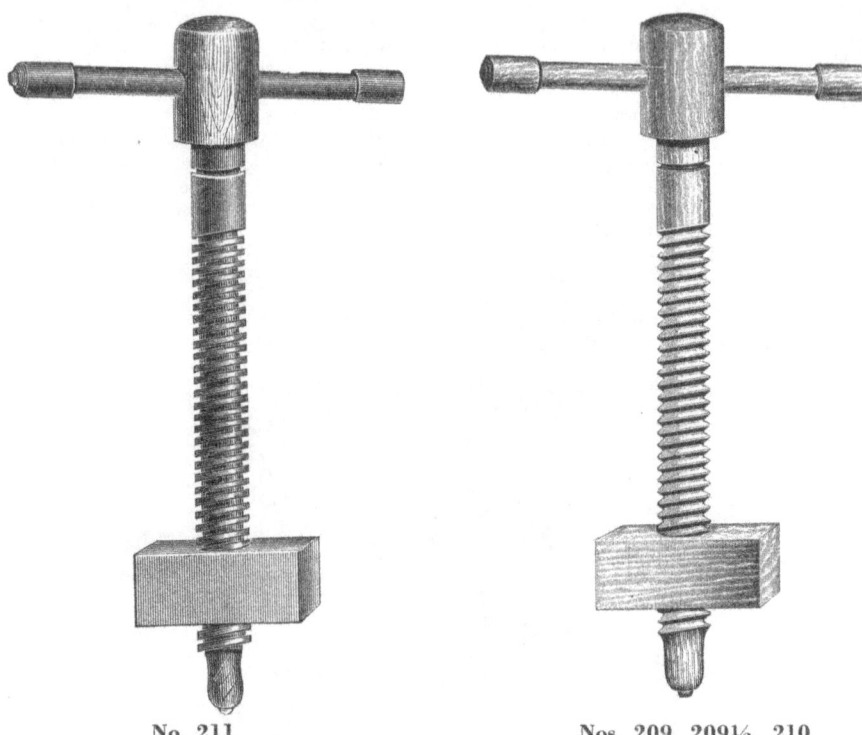

No. 211   Nos. 209, 209½, 210
                              211¼ and 211½

Stock No.	Description	Price per Dozen.
209	Hard Maple Bench Screws, V-Thread, 2"x24"	$16.70
209½	Hard Maple Bench Screws, V-Thread, 2¼"x24"	17.00
210	Hard Maple Bench Screws, V-Thread, 2½"x24"	17.70
211	Hard Maple Bench Screws, Square Thread, 2½"x24"	21.40
211¼	Hickory Bench Screws, V-Thread, 2"x24"	21.40
211½	Hickory Bench Screws, V-Thread, 2½"x24"	22.70
211¾	Hard Maple Tail Screws, 2" to 2½"x24"	32.00

Packed Two Dozen in a Case.

IMPORTANT NOTICE

Our Wood Hand Screws and Bench Screws are guaranteed to be made of thoroughly seasoned timber, and to be perfect in every respect when they leave our plant. We will replace, free of charge, or repair and place in first-class order, all those which were obviously not perfect at the time of shipment. We cannot, however, replace Hand or Bench Screws which were ruined by misuse, by being varnished or painted, or by being kept in damp or overheated places.

It must always be borne in mind that these screws are made of *wood* and not of iron or steel. They should, consequently, never be tightened with a wrench, nor tightened to an unreasonable tension by hand. When we have Hand or Bench Screws returned to us which show obvious indications of such misuse, we regret that we must decline to replace them.

Wood Hand or Bench Screws should never be painted, oiled, or covered with any foreign substance, as this is liable to cause swelling and ruin the threads. Moreover, the most perfectly seasoned wood in the world will warp and swell if exposed to the weather, or if kept in a damp or overheated place, and we cannot hold ourselves responsible for such occurence. They should always be kept in moderate temperatures, and in dry places.

In using Wood Hand Screws, the danger of stripping threads is minimized if the spindles are always kept at perfect right angles to the jaws. The square shoulder or set screw should be tightened first, and the round shoulder or push screw afterwards.

Flask Clamps

(Hard Maple Bars, Hickory Screws)

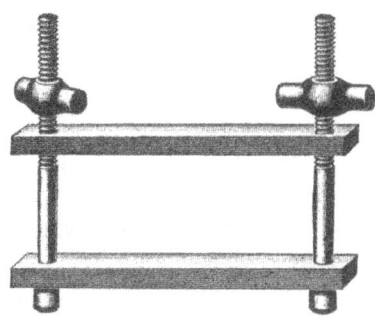

Size No.		Price per Dozen
0	12″ between screws; 2½″ wide; 1″ thick; screws, 15″ under head, 1″ diameter; nuts, 6″ long......................	$30.00
1	16″ between screws; 2¾″ wide; 1¼″ thick; screws, 16″ under head, 1¼″ diameter; nuts, 6″ long......................	33.60
2	16¾″ between screws; 2¾″ wide; 1⅜″ thick; screws, 16″ under head, 1¼″ diameter; nuts 8½″ long.............	33.60
3	18″ between screws; 2¾″ wide; 1⅜″ thick; screws, 16″ under head; 1¼″ diameter; nuts 8½″ long.............	36.00

Wood Cabinet Maker's Clamps

Stock No.		Price per Doz:
224A	Cabinet Maker's Clamps, length inside jaws, 3 ft.	$24.00
224B	Cabinet Maker's Clamps, length inside jaws, 4 ft.	30.00
224C	Cabinet Maker's Clamps, length inside jaws, 5 ft.	36.00

"Sandusky" Wood Planes

Wood Planes have always been preferred by expert woodworkers for work requiring extreme accuracy, such as pattern, cabinet, and furniture making, etc. Furthermore, a wood plane can be used on green timber or extremely hard wood with considerably less friction, and consequently with less effort, than any other type of plane known, and this feature appeals to workmen using planes for long periods at a time. The well-known durability of wood planes, and the fact that they are lower-priced than any other kinds of planes, are likewise very important factors from the standpoint of the purchaser.

Our line of wood planes is the largest and most complete made by any concern in the world. We manufacture wood planes for every conceivable purpose for which a plane could be used, and in addition to the very complete line illustrated and described in this catalog, we are prepared to make special planes for special purposes in any quantities.

Our wood planes are made from carefully-selected, air-seasoned, Ohio Second-Growth White Beech, the finest plane timber known, both from the standpoint of durability and appearance, and infinitely superior to the relatively soft European White Beech from which foreign-made planes are manufactured. The planes are sawed out radially from the tough-textured sapwood of the logs, which results in the annual rings beings parallel with the bases of the planes. This prevents warping, and insures the planes' wearing evenly instead of on an angle, which is the case with planes made from plank.

The workmanship in all of our wood planes is unexcelled, and they are fully warranted in every respect.

All "Sandusky" Planes are equipped with our famous, thick, wedge-shaped plane irons or cutters, which are recognized as the finest obtainable.

"Sandusky" Wood Planes have been known as the finest on the market for sixty years, and have won high awards at innumerable expositions, including the Gold Medal at the Philadelphia Centennial Exposition in 1876.

"Sandusky" Wood Bench Planes

Smoothing Planes

(8″ Long)

(Width of Irons, 1½″ to 2¼″, by eighths)

(All with Polished Lignum Vitae Starts)

(Packed 36 in a Case)

	No. 1 and 3	No. 5	

Stock No:		Price Each:
1	Single-Iron Smoothing Plane	$1.60
3	Double-Iron Smoothing Plane	2.00
4	Double-Iron Carriage Smoothing Plane, 1½″—Iron	2.00
5	Double-Iron Smoothing Plane, with Solid Handle	3.90
5½	Double-Iron Smoothing Plane, with Jack Handle	3.40

For Smoothing Planes with extra sized Single Irons, add ten cents each; with extra sized Double Irons, add twenty cents each.

Smoothing Planes, without irons $1.40

Jack Planes

(16″ Long)

(Width of Irons, 2″, 2⅛″, & 2¼″)

(All with Polished Lignum Vitae Starts)

(Packed 36 in a Case)

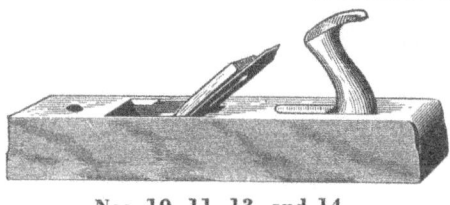
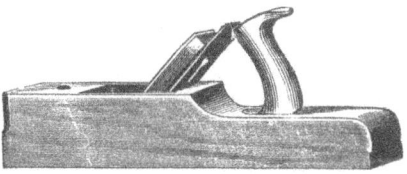

	Nos. 10, 11, 13, and 14	Nos. 12 and 15	

Stock No:		Price Each:
10	Single-Iron Jack Plane	$1.80
11	Single-Iron Jack Planes, with Bolted Handle	2.50
12	Single-Iron Jack Plane, with Razee Handle	2.50
13	Double-Iron Jack Plane	2.30
14	Double-Iron Jack Plane, with Bolted Handle	2.40
15	Double-Iron Jack Plane, with Razee Handle	2.70

For Jack Planes with extra sized Single Irons, add ten cents each; with extra sized Double Irons, add twenty cents each.

Jack Planes, without irons $1.60

Fore Planes

(22″ Long)
(Width of Irons, 2⅜″, & 2½″)
(All with Polished Lignum Vitae Starts)
(Packed 24 in a Case)

Stock No.	Nos. 16, 17, 19 and 20	Price per Doz:
16	Single-Iron Fore Plane	$3.20
17	Single-Iron Fore Plane, with Bolted Handle	3.80
18	Single-Iron Fore Plane, with Razee Handle	3.80
19	Double-Iron Fore Plane	3.80
20	Double-Iron Fore Plane, with Bolted Handle	4.00
21	Double-Iron Fore Plane, with Razee Handle	4.30

For Fore Planes with extra sized Single Irons, add ten cents each; with extra sized Double Irons, add twenty cents each.

Fore Planes, without irons 3.00

Jointer Planes

(24″ to 30″ Long)
(Width of Irons, 2½″)
(All with Polished Lignum Vitae Starts)
(Packed 20 in a Case)

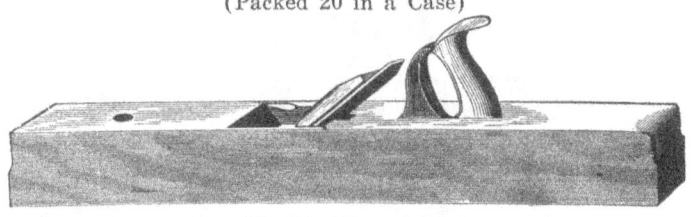

Nos. 22, 23, 25, and 26

Stock No.		24″	26″	28″	Price Each 30″
22	Single-Iron Jointer Plane	$3.40	$3.40	$3.60	$4.00
23	Single-Iron Jointer Plane, with Bolted Handle		26″ $4.40	28″ $4.60	30″ $5.00
24	Single-Iron Jointer Plane, with Razee Handle		26″ $4.00	28″ $4.30	30″ $4.70
25	Double-Iron Jointer Plane	24″ $4.00	26″ $4.00	28″ $4.30	30″ $4.80
26	Double-Iron Jointer Plane, with Bolted Handle		26″ $4.20	28″ $4.40	30″ $5.00
27	Double-Iron Jointer Plane, with Razee Handle		26″ $4.60	28″ $4.80	30″ $5.40

For Jointer Planes with extra sized Single Irons, add ten cents each; with extra sized Double Irons, add twenty cents each.

	24″	26″	28″	30″
Jointer Planes, without irons	$3.20	$3.20	$3.30	$3.80

Selected Applewood Bench Planes

Stock No:		Price Each:
28	Double-Iron Applewood Smoothing Plane, 1½″ to 2¼″	$3.40
29	Double-Iron Applewood Smoothing Plane, 1½″ to 2¼″, with Solid Handle	5.00
30	Double-Iron Applewood Jack Plane, 2″ to 2¼″, with Bolted Handle	3.90
31	Double-Iron Applewood Fore Plane, 2⅜″ to 2½″, with Bolted Handle	5.40
32	Double-Iron Applewood Jointer Plane, 26″, 2½″, with Bolted Handle	7.20
33	Single-Iron Applewood Smoothing Plane, 1½″ to 2¼″	3.00
34	Single-Iron Applewood Jack Plane, 2″ to 2¼″, with Bolted Handle	3.40
35	Single-Iron Applewood Fore Plane, 2⅜″ to 2½″, with Bolted Handle	4.70
35½	Single-Iron Applewood Jointer Plane, 26″, 2½″, with Bolted Handle	5.80

Boxwood and Rosewood Planes made to order.

Aluminum-Top Bench Planes

These planes are the lighest-weight planes we manufacture, and are especially adapted to the requirements of pattern-makers and other wood-workers desiring light planes for work of great precision.

The wood parts of these planes are made of selected, air-seasoned native white beech, and are carefully finished and varnished. The irons are the same as used in our all-wood planes, and are full-polished.

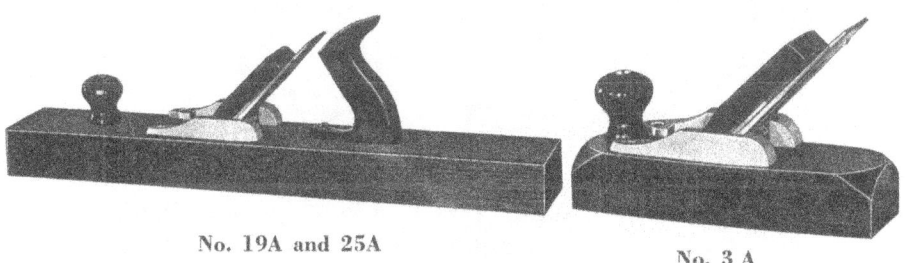

No. 19A and 25A

No. 3 A

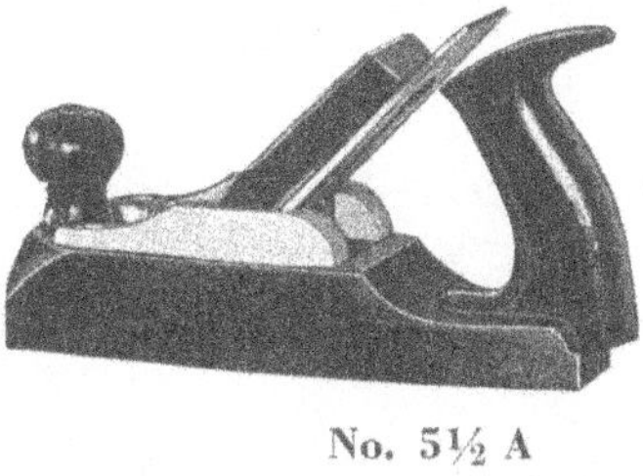

No. 5½ A

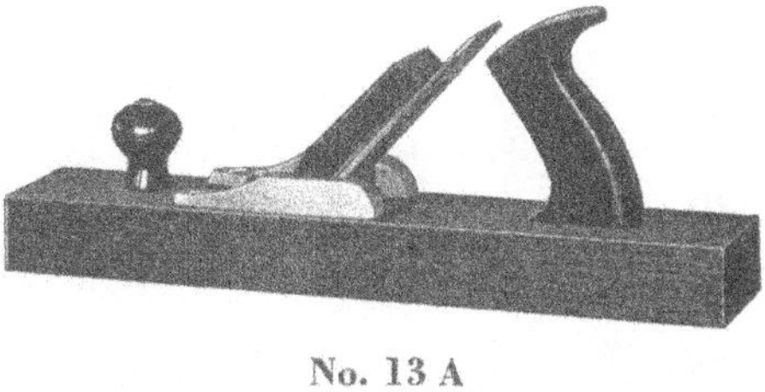

No. 13 A

Aluminum-Top Bench Planes—(Continued)

Stock No:				Price Each:
3	A	Double-Iron, Aluminum-Top Smoothing Plane, 7″ to 8″ Long, 1¾″ to 2″ Iron		$2.40
5½	A	Double-Iron, Aluminum-Top Smoothing Plane, with Jack Handle, 9″ Long, 2″ Iron		3.40
13	A	Double-Iron, Aluminum-Top Jack Plane, 15″ Long, 2″ to 2¼″ Iron		2.80
19	A	Double-Iron, Aluminum-Top Fore Plane, 18″ and 20″ Long, 2⅜″ Iron		4.00
25	A	Double-Iron, Aluminum-Top Jointer Plane,	22″ and 24″ Long, 2⅜″ Iron	4.30
			26″ and 28″ Long, 2⅝″ Iron	4.60
			30″ Long, 2⅝″ Iron	5.00

Selected Beech Planes

Made from extra fine, second-growth white beech sapwood, air-seasoned for four years. The plane blocks are very carefully finished, and are polished and waxed by hand.

No. XX Bench Planes

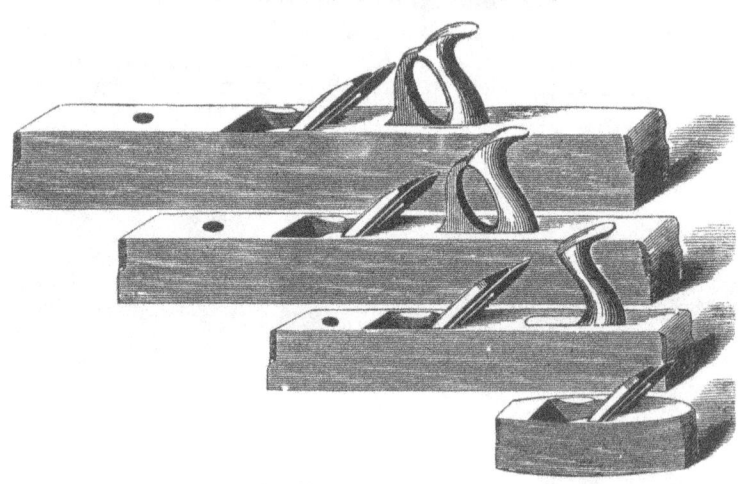

	Price Each:		Price Each
Single-Iron Smoothing Plane	$ 3.00	Double-Iron Smoothing Plane	$3.40
Single-Iron Jack Plane	3.60	Double-Iron Jack Plane	4.10
Single-Iron Fore Plane	4.50	Double-Iron Fore Plane	5.00
Single-Iron Jointer Plane, 26″	5.20	Double-Iron Jointer Plane, 26″	5.80
Per set of four planes	$16.30	Per set of four planes	$18.30

No. 02 Ship Planes

No satisfactory substitute has ever been found for wood planes in shipbuilding work. They are far less fatiguing to the user than other types of planes, as they will slide over oak, ash, and other hard woods with a minimum of friction.

Price Each:

	Price Each:
Double-Iron Smooth Plane, 9" Long, 1¾" to 2" Iron	$2.30
Double-Iron Jack Plane, 16" Long, 1¾" to 2⅛" Iron, with Razee Handle	2.70
Double-Iron Fore Plane, 22" Long, 2" to 2¼" Iron, with Razee Handle	4.30
Double-Iron Jointer Plane, 26" Long, 2¼" to 2½" Iron, with Razee Handle	4.70
Per set of four planes	$14.00

No. 05 Selected Beech Bench Planes

With Razee Handles

	Price Each		Price Each
Single-Iron Jack Plane	$2.60	Double-Iron Jack Plane	$2.80
Single-Iron Fore Plane	3.90	Double-Iron Fore Plane	4.40
Single-Iron Jointer Plane	4.20	Double-Iron Jointer Plane	4.70
Per set of three planes	$10.70	Per set of three planes	$11.90

No. 06 Horned Smoothing, Jack, and Scrub Planes

Single-Iron Horned Smoothing Plane, 8½" Long, 1½" to 2¼" Iron $2.70
Single-Iron Horned Jack Plane, 16" Long, 1½" to 2¼" Iron..... 3.20
Double-Iron Horned Smoothing Plane, 8½" Long, 1½" to 2¼"
    Iron.. 2.80
Double-Iron Horned Jack Plane, 16" Long, 1½" to 2¼" Iron.... 3.30
Single-Iron Horned Scrub Plane, 8½" Long, 1¼"; 1⅜" and 1½"
    Iron.. 2.80

Miscellaneous Planes

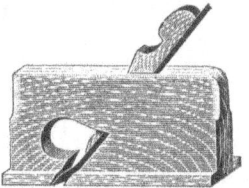

No. 39 Mitre Plane	No. 045A T-Rabbet Plane	Nos. 045 B, C, & D Oar and Spar Plane

Stock No:		Price Each:
36	Beech Tooth Plane, 2⅛" Iron	$3.20
37	Applewood Tooth Plane, 2⅛" Iron	4.00
38	Single-Iron Square Mitre Plane	3.00
38½	Single-Iron Smooth-Shape Mitre Plane	2.50
39	Double-Iron Smooth-Shape Mitre Plane	3.20
41	Gutter Plane	4.00
42	Pump Plane (For Chain Pumps)	6.00
43	Pump Plane, with Handle	7.50
44	Single-Iron Circular or Heel Plane	4.00
45	Double-Iron Circular or Heel Plane	5.00
45½	Double-Iron Box Maker's Jack Plane, with Razee Handle	4.00
045½	Single-Iron Box Maker's Jack Plane, with Razee Handle	4.50
045¾	Single-Iron Box Maker's Smooth Plane	3.00
045A	Carriage Maker's T-Rabbet Plane	3.50
045B	Single-Iron Smooth-Shape Oar Plane	6.00
045B	Double-Iron Smooth-Shape Oar Plane	7.00
045C	Single-Iron Smooth-Shape Spar Plane	6.00
045C	Double-Iron Smooth-Shape Spar Plane	7.00

Astragals

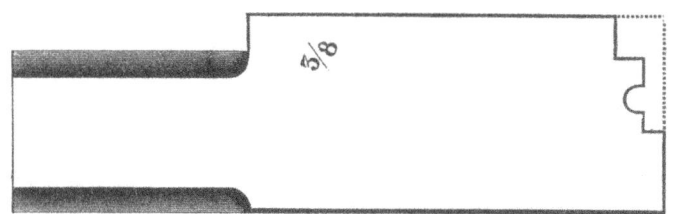

Stock No:		Price Each:
46 Astragals....................	$\frac{3}{8}''$ to $1''$	$3.50
	$1\frac{1}{8}''$ to $1\frac{1}{4}''$	4.00

Side Bead Planes

Stock 'No:		Price Each:
47 Single-Boxed Side Bead Planes	$\frac{1}{8}''$, $\frac{3}{16}''$, $\frac{1}{4}''$ $\frac{5}{16}''$, $\frac{3}{8}''$ and $\frac{1}{2}''$	$1.70
	$\frac{5}{8}''$ and $\frac{3}{4}''$	1.90
	$\frac{7}{8}''$ and $1''$	2.20
	$1\frac{1}{4}''$	2.60
	$1\frac{1}{2}''$	3.00

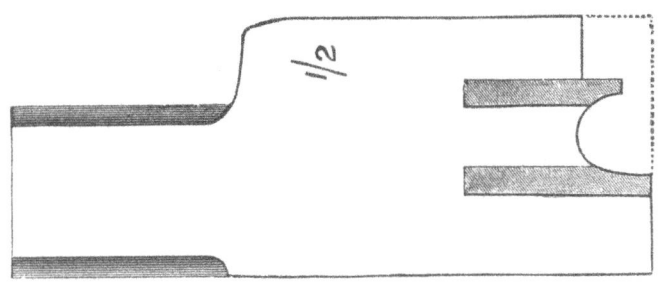

Stock No:		Price Each:
48 Double-Boxed Side Bead Planes	$\frac{1}{8}''$, $\frac{3}{16}''$, $\frac{1}{4}''$, $\frac{5}{16}''$ $\frac{3}{8}''$ and $\frac{1}{2}''$	$2.00
	$\frac{5}{8}''$ and $\frac{3}{4}''$	2.20
	$\frac{7}{8}''$ and $1''$	2.50
	$1\frac{1}{4}''$	2.90
	$1\frac{1}{2}''$	3.30

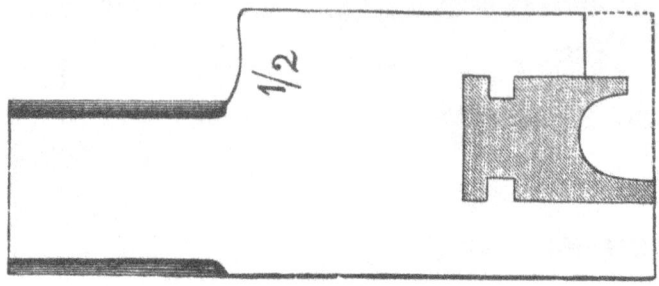

49 Solid-Boxed, Dovetailed, Side

Bead Planes................. $\frac{1}{8}''$, $\frac{3}{16}''$, $\frac{1}{4}''$ and $\frac{5}{16}''$ $2.20

$\frac{3}{8}''$ and $\frac{1}{2}''$ 2.50

$\frac{5}{8}''$ and $\frac{3}{4}''$ 2.60

$\frac{7}{8}''$ and $1''$ 2.90

For Twin Bead Planes, to work right and left, double list price for single plane.

Center Bead Planes

Stock No: Size: Price Each:

51 Double-Boxed Center Bead Plane

$\frac{1}{8}''$, 3/16″, $\frac{1}{4}''$, 5/16″, $\frac{3}{8}''$ & $\frac{1}{2}''$ $2.00

$\frac{5}{8}''$ and $\frac{3}{4}''$ 2.20

$\frac{7}{8}''$ and $1''$ 2.50

52 Solid-Boxed, Dovetailed, Center Bead Plane

$\frac{1}{8}''$, 3/16″, $\frac{1}{4}''$, 5/16″ & $\frac{3}{8}''$ 2.40

$\frac{1}{2}''$, $\frac{5}{8}''$, and $\frac{3}{4}''$ 2.60

Torus Bead Planes

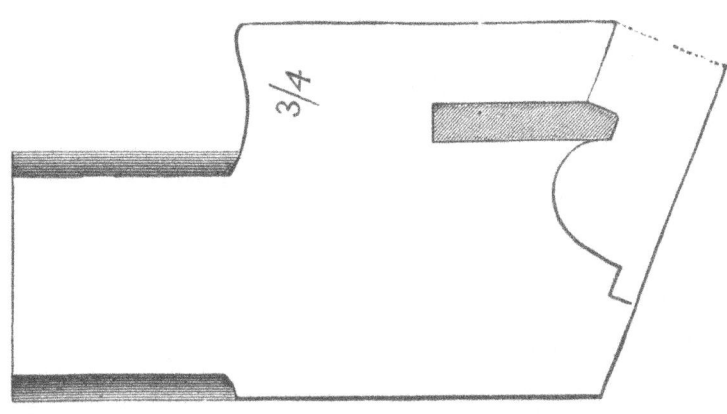

Stock No:		Size:	Price Each:
52½	Torus Bead Plane	⅜″, ½″, ⅝″, ¾″, ⅞″ & 1″	$3.50

Cove Planes

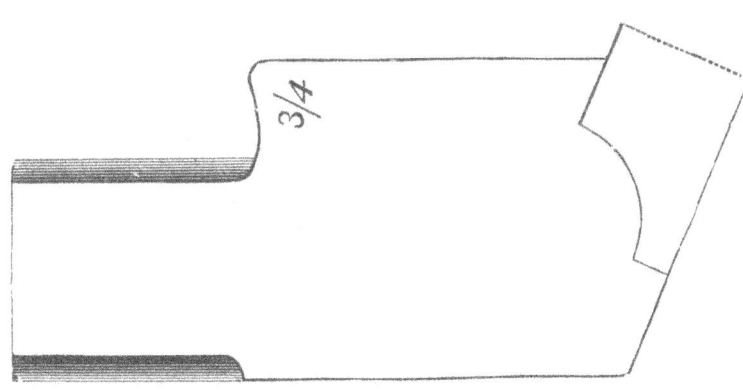

Stock No:		Size:	Price Each:
53	Cove Plane	½″, ⅝″, and ¾″	$2.50
		⅞″ and 1″	3.00
		1¼″	3.50

Scotia or Quarter-Round Planes

Stock No.		Size	Price Each
54	Scotia or Quarter-Round Plane	⅜". ½" and ⅝"	$2.50
		¾", ⅞" and 1"	3.00
		1¼"	3.50

Quarter-Round or Casing Moulding Planes

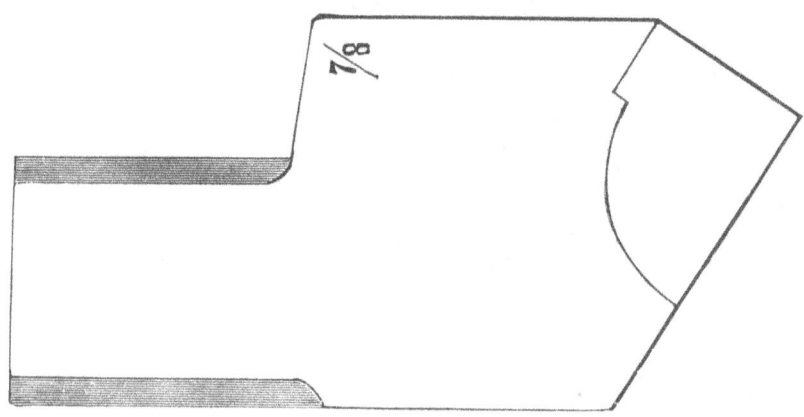

Stock No.		Size	Price Each
54½	Quarter-Round or Casing Moulding Planes...........	⅜", ½" and ⅝"	$2.50
		¾", ⅞" and 1"	3.00
		1¼"	3.50

Casting Moulding Planes, with Fence

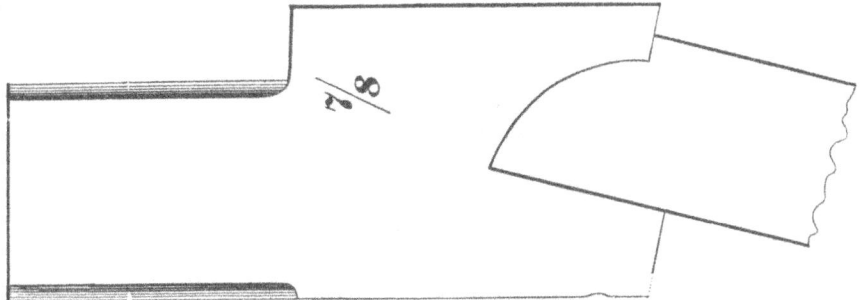

This is an improved style of plane for cutting the same moulding as No. 54½. The plane is made to work on a slight spring, and the iron is skewed, making the plane much easier to operate than the older type.

Stock No.		Size	Price Each
54¾	Casing Moulding Plane, with Fence....................	½″, ⅝″ and ¾″	$3.00
		⅞″ and 1″	3.30
		1¼″	3.60

Cove and Bead Planes

Stock No.		Size	Price Each
55	Cove and Bead Plane.........	½″, ⅝″ and ¾″	$4.00
		⅞″ and 1″	4.50
		1¼″	5.00

Coping Planes

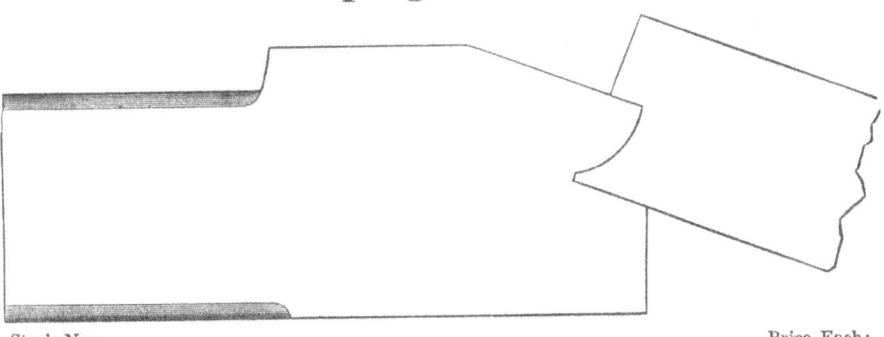

Stock No:		Price Each:
56	Coping Plane for Sash Planes	$2.50
57	Coping Plane, Boxed, for Sash Planes	3.00
58	Coping Plane for Doors	3.00

Dado Planes

No. 62

Stock No:		Size:	Price Each:
60	Dado Plane, with Brass Side-Stop	¼" to 1" by eighths	$3.20
61	Dado Plane, with Brass Screw-Stop and Solid Handle	¼" to 1" by eighths	7.30
62	Dado Plane, with Brass Screw-Stop	¼" to 1" by eighths	4.40

Filletster Planes

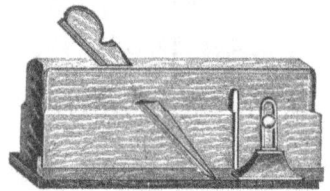

No. 68

Stock No:		Price Each:
65	Plain Filletster Plane	$3.20
66	Filletster Plane, with Cutter	3.60
67	Filletster Plane, with Cutter and Brass Side-Stop	4.00
68	Filletster Plane, with Cutter, Brass Side-Stop and Boxed	5.30
69	Filletster Plane, with Cutter, Brass Screw-Stop and Boxed	7.00
70	Filletster Plane, with Cutter, Brass Screw-Stop, Boxed, and with Boxwood Fence	8.40
71	Filletster Plane, with Cutter, Brass Screw-Stop, Boxed and with Boxwood Screw-Arms	11.00
72	Filletster Plane, with Cutter, Brass Screw-Stop, Boxed, with Boxwood Screw-Arms, and Handle	13.30
73	Back Filletster Plane, with Screw Arms	9.90

Common Ogee Planes

Stock No.		Size	Price Each
74	Common Ogee Plane..........	½", ¾" and 1"	$2.00
		1¼" and 1½"	2.30
		1¾" and 2"	2.60

Grecian Ogee Planes, with Quirk and Bead

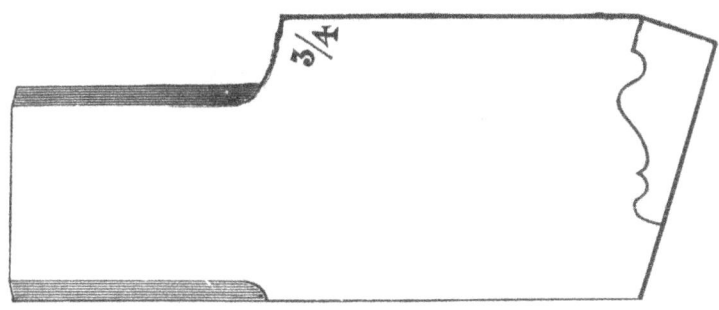

Stock No.		Size	Price Each
75	Grecian Ogee Plane, with Quirk and Bead.................	¾" and 1"	$4.00
		1¼"	4.50
		1½"	5.00
		1¾"	5.50
		2"	6.00

Roman Ogee Planes

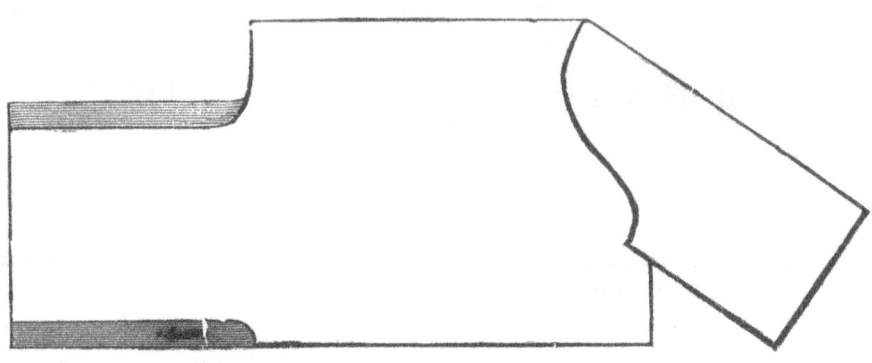

Stock No.		Size	Price Each
76	Roman Ogee Plane, To Work on	$\frac{3}{8}''$ and $\frac{1}{2}''$	$2.20
	Edge..................	$\frac{5}{8}''$, $\frac{3}{4}''$, $\frac{7}{8}''$ and $1''$	2.50

Grecian Ogee Planes

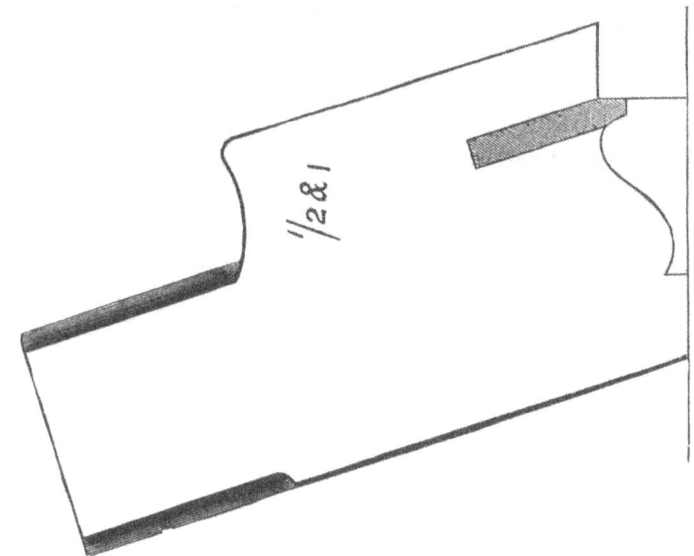

77	Grecian Ogee Plane	$\frac{1}{2}''$, $\frac{3}{4}''$, and $1''$	$2.20
		$1\frac{1}{4}''$ and $1\frac{1}{2}''$	2.60
		$1\frac{3}{4}''$ and $2''$	3.00
	With Handle, add		1.20

Grecian Ogee Plane With Bead

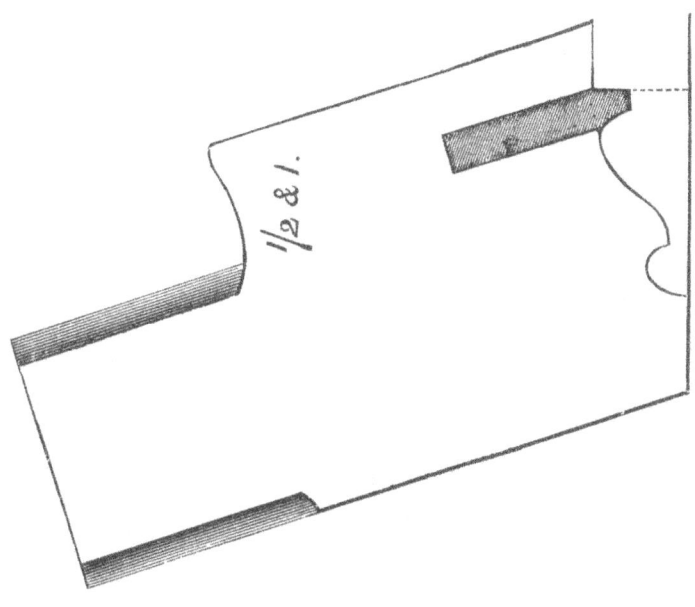

Stock No:		Size:	Price Each:
78	Grecian Ogee Plane with Bead	½″, ¾″, and 1″	$2.60
		1¼″ and 1½″	2.90
		1¾″ and 2″	3.50
	With Handle, add		1.20

Grecian Ogee Plane With Bevel

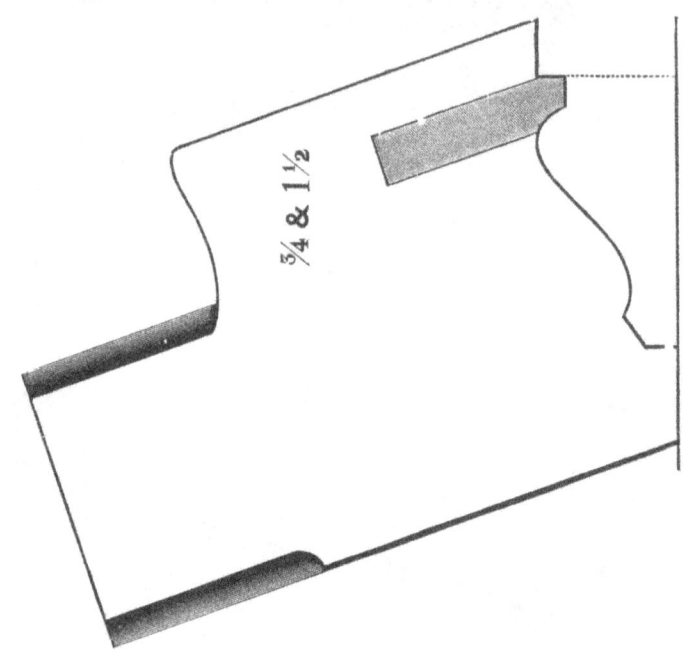

Stock No:		Size:	Price Each:
79	Grecian Ogee Plane with Bevel or Fillet	½", ¾", and 1"	$2.60
		1¼" and 1½"	2.90
		1¾" and 2"	3.50
	With Handle, add		1.20

Cabinet and Cornice Ogee Planes

Stock No:		Size:	Price Per Inch
80	Cabinet Maker's Ogee Plane	2" to 4"	$4.00
80½	Cornice Ogee Plane	2" to 4"	4.00

Reverse Ogee Planes

Stock No:	Size:	Price Each:
81 Reverse Ogee Plane	¾″ and 1″	$2.20
	1¼″ and 1½″	2.50
	1¾″ and 2″	3.00
	2¼″ and 2½″	3.50
With Handle, add		1.20

Roman Reverse Ogee Planes

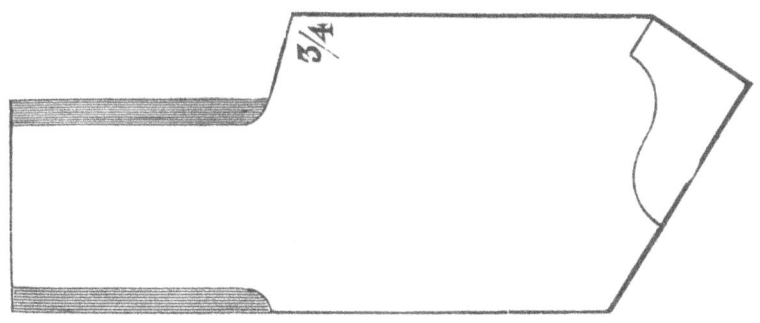

Stock No:	Size:	Price Each:
82 Roman Reverse Ogee Plane	⅜″ and ½″	$2.20
	¾″ and 1″	2.50
	1¼″	3.00
	1½″ and 1¾″	3.40

Roman Reverse Ogee Planes, With Fence

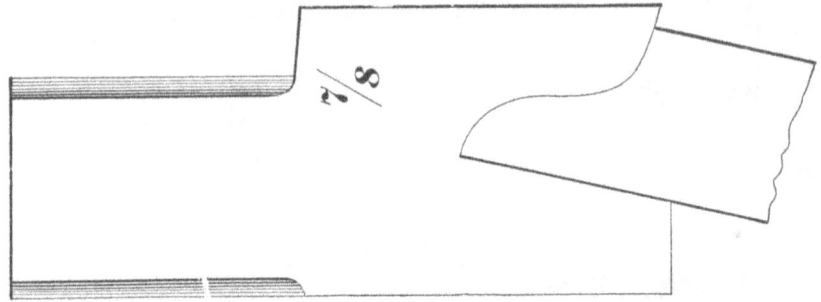

This is an improved style of plane for cutting the same moulding as No. 82. The plane is made to work on a slight spring, and the iron is skewed, making the plane much easier to operate than the older type.

Stock No:	Size:	Price Each:
82½ Roman Reverse Ogee Plane, with Fence		
	⅜″, ½″, and ⅝″	$2.30
	¾″, ⅞″, and 1″	2.60
	1¼″	3.00

Grecian Ovolo Plane, With Square

Stock No:	Size:	Price Each:
83 Grecian Ovolo Plane, with Square.....	½″, ¾″, and 1″	$2.60
	1¼″ and 1½″	2.90
	1¾″ and 2″	3.50
	2¼″ and 2½″	4.20
With Handle, add		1.20

Grecian Ovolo Plane, With Fillet

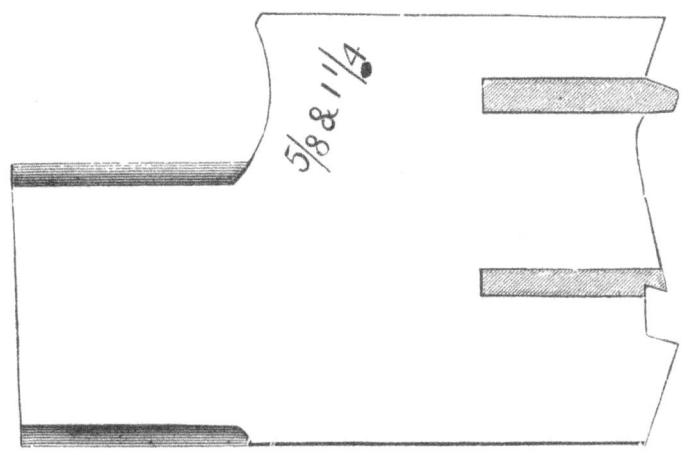

Stock No:		Size:	Price Each:
84	Grecian Ovolo Plane, with Bevel or Fillet		
		¾″ and 1″	$3.00
		1¼″ and 1½″	3.50
		1¾″ and 2″	4.00
	With Handle, add		1.20

Grecian Ovolo Plane, With Bead

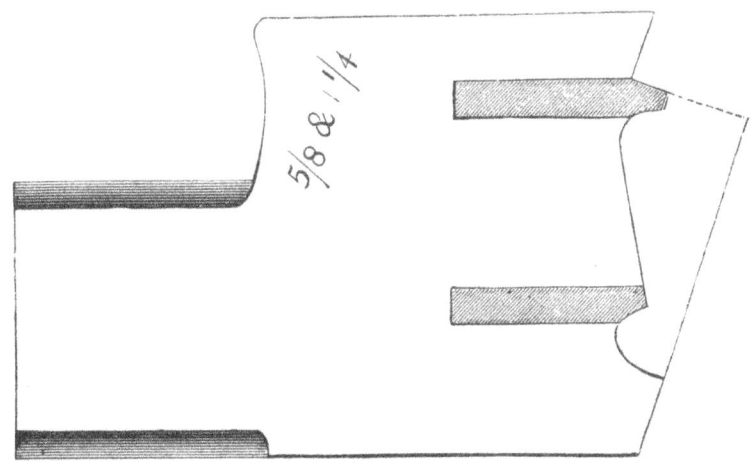

Stock No:		Size:	Price Each:
85	Grecian Ovolo Plane, with Bead	¾″ and 1″	$3.00
		1¼″ and 1½″	3.50
		1¾″ and 2″	4.00
	With Handle, add		1.20

Hollow and Round Planes

No. 92. One Set

Nos. 1-9

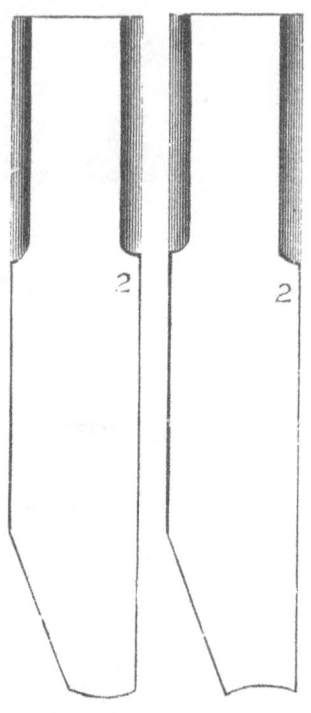

One Pair No. 2

No. 92 Hollow and Round Planes

Size No.	Size	Diameter of Circle on Which Plane Works	Price Each	Price per Pair
1	¼ "	½ "	$1.60	$3.20
2	⅜ "	¾ "	1.60	3.20
3	½ "	1 "	1.60	3.20
4	⅝ "	1 ¼ "	1.60	3.20
5	¾ "	1 ½ "	1.60	3.20
6	⅞ "	1 ¾ "	1.60	3.20
7	1 "	2 "	1.80	3.60
8	1 ⅛ "	2 ¼ "	1.80	3.60
9	1 ¼ "	2 ½ "	1.80	3.60

No. 94 Hollow and Round Planes

Size No.	Size	Diameter of Circle on Which Plane Works	Price Each	Price per Pair
10	1 ⅜ "	2 ¾ "	2.00	4.00
11	1 ½ "	3 "	2.00	4.00
12	1 ⅝ "	3 ¼ "	2.00	4.00
13	1 ¾ "	3 ½ "	2.30	4.60
14	1 ⅞ "	3 ¾ "	2.30	4.60
15	2 "	4 "	2.30	4.60

No. 95 Skewed Hollow and Round Planes

Same Sizes, and Prices as Nos. 92 and 94 Square Hollow and Round Planes.

Reverse Ogee Plane, with Square

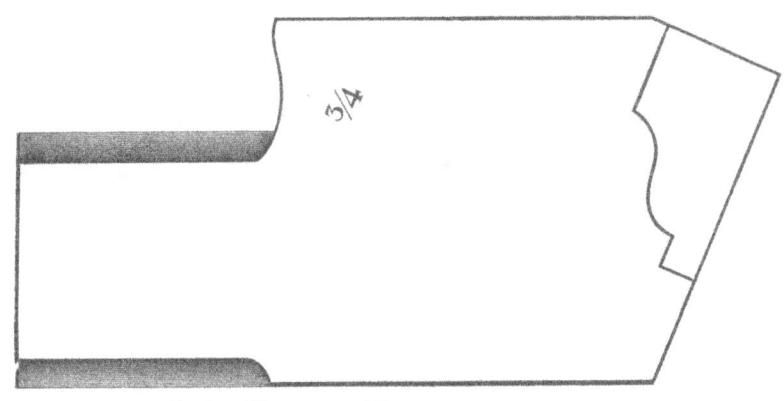

96	Reverse Ogee Plane, with Square	½″	$2.20
		¾″ and 1″	2.50
		1¼″	3.00
		1½″, 1¾″ and 2″	3.30

Door Ogee Plane

Stock No:		Size:	Price Each:
97	Door Moulding Plane	½″, ¾″, 1″, and 1¼″	$2.60
		1½″, 1¾″, and 2″	3.00

Match Planes

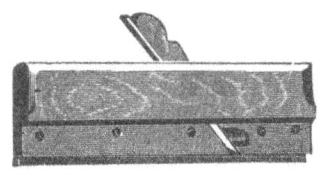 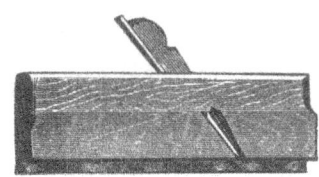

One Pair No. 99

Stock No.		Size	Price per Pair
98½	Board Match Planes, Twin or Separate	¼″	$7.00
99	Board Match Planes, Twin or Separate	⅜″, ½″, ⅝″, ¾″, ⅞″ and 1″	4.40
99½	Board Match Planes, Separate	1¼″ and 1½″	5.20
99¾	Board Match Planes, Twin or Separate, Plated	¼″	9.50
100	Board Match Planes, Twin or Separate, Plated	⅜″, ½″, ⅝″, ¾″, ⅞″ and 1″	5.00
100½	Board Match Planes, Separate, Plated	1¼″ and 1½″	5.80

(Nos. 98½ and 99¾ are made entirely by hand).

One Pair No. 101—Handled Match Planes

Stock No.		Size	Price per Pair
101	Board Match Planes, With Solid Handles.............	$\frac{3}{8}$", $\frac{1}{2}$", $\frac{5}{8}$", $\frac{3}{4}$", $\frac{7}{8}$" and 1"	$6.00
101½	Board Match Planes, With Solid Handles.............	1¼" and 1½"	7.20
102	Board Match Planes, With Solid Handles, Plated.....	$\frac{3}{8}$", $\frac{1}{2}$", $\frac{5}{8}$", $\frac{3}{4}$" $\frac{7}{8}$" and 1"	6.60
102½	Board Match Planes, with Solid Handles, Plated....	1¼" and 1½"	7.80

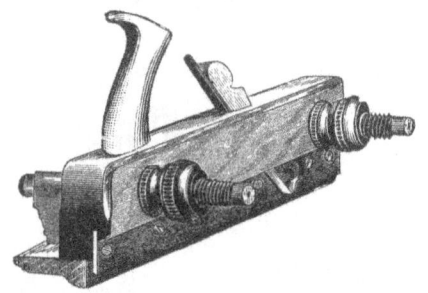

No. 106—To Work Groove

Stock No.		Size	Price per Pair
103	Plank Match Planes	1¼" and 1½"	$6.00
104	Plank Match Planes, Plated	1¼" and 1½"	6.60
105	Plank Match Planes, Boxed	1¼" and 1½"	6.60
106	Plank Match Planes, with Screw Arms		10.00
106½	Plank Match Planes, with Screw Arms, plated		10.70
107	Plank Match Planes, with Screw Arms, boxed		11.30
108	Plank Match Planes, with Screw Arms, plated & boxed		12.00
109	Plank Match Planes, with Screw Arms, full plated		12.80

Nosing Planes

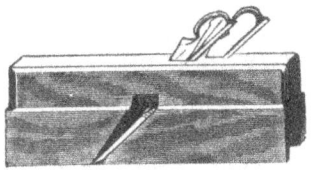

No. 113

Stock No.		Size	Price Each
110	Nosing Moulding Plane.......	$\frac{1}{2}''$	$2.50
		$\frac{3}{4}''$	2.80
		1'' and 1 $\frac{1}{4}''$	3.00
		1 $\frac{1}{2}''$	3.50
111	Nosing Plane, With One Iron.	$\frac{3}{4}''$, $\frac{7}{8}''$, 1'', 1 $\frac{1}{8}''$ and 1 $\frac{1}{4}''$	2.50
		1 $\frac{3}{8}''$ and 1 $\frac{1}{2}''$	3.00
		1 $\frac{3}{4}''$ and 2''	3.50
112	Nosing Plane, With One Iron and Handle..............	1'', 1 $\frac{1}{8}''$ and 1 $\frac{1}{4}''$	3.20
		1 $\frac{3}{8}''$ and 1 $\frac{1}{2}''$	3.70
		1 $\frac{3}{4}''$ and 2''	4.20
113	Nosing Plane, With Two Irons	$\frac{3}{4}''$, $\frac{7}{8}''$, 1'', 1 $\frac{1}{8}''$ and 1 $\frac{1}{4}''$	3.20
		1 $\frac{3}{8}''$ and 1 $\frac{1}{2}''$	3.70
		1 $\frac{3}{4}''$ and 2''	4.20
114	Nosing Plane, with Two Irons and Handle..............	1'', 1 $\frac{1}{8}''$ and 1 $\frac{1}{4}''$	4.20
		1 $\frac{3}{8}''$ and 1 $\frac{1}{2}''$	4.90
		1 $\frac{3}{4}''$ and 2''	5.60

Panel Plows

Stock No:		Price Each:
116	Beech Panel Plow, with Four Irons and Wood Stop, Without Handle	$8.00
117	Beech Panel Plow, with Eight Irons and Screw Stop, Without Handle	11.00
118	Beech Panel Plow, with Eight Irons, Screw Stop, and Boxed Fence, without Handle	11.70

119	Beech Panel Plow, with Eight Irons, Screw Stop, and Handle	13.00
120	Beech Panel Plow, with Eight Irons, Screw Stop, Boxed Fence and Handle	13.70
121	Beech Panel Plow, with Eight Irons, Screw Stop, Boxwood Arms, without Handle	12.50
122	Beech Panel Plow, with Eight Irons, Screw Stop, Boxwood Arms, Boxed Fence, without Handle	13.20
123	Beech Panel Plow, with Eight Irons, Screw Stop, Boxwood Arms, and Handle	15.50
124	Beech Panel Plow, with Eight Irons, Screw Stop, Boxwood Arms, Boxed Fence, and Handle	16.00
125	Applewood Panel Plow, with Eight Irons, Screw Stop, Boxed Fence, and Handle	15.50
126	Applewood Panel Plow, with Eight Irons, Screw Stop, Boxwood Arms, without Handle	$15.00
127	Applewood Panel Plow, with Eight Irons, Screw Stop, Boxwood Arms, Boxed Fence, without Handle	16.00
128	Applewood Panel Plow, with Eight Irons, Screw Stop, Boxwood Arms, and Handle	18.00
129	Applewood Panel Plow, with Eight Irons, Screw Stop, Boxwood Arms, Boxed Fence, and Handle	18.50
130	Boxwood or Rosewood Panel Plow, with Eight Irons, Screw Stop, without Handle	16.00
131	Boxwood or Rosewood Panel Plow, Ivory-Tipped, with Eight Irons, Screw Stop, without Handle	18.00
132	Boxwood or Rosewood Panel Plow, with Eight Irons, Screw Stop, and Handle	20.00
133	Boxwood or Rosewood Panel Plow, Ivory-Tipped, with Eight Irons, Screw Stop, and Handle	22.00
134	Ebony Panel Plow, with Eight Irons, Screw Stop, without Handle	20.00
135	Ebony Panel Plow, Ivory-Tipped, with Eight Irons, Screw Stop, without Handle	22.00
136	Ebony Panel Plow, with Eight Irons, Screw Stop, and Handle	24.00
137	Ebony Panel Plow, Ivory-Tipped, with Eight Irons, Screw Stop, and Handle	26.00
138	Boxwood or Rosewood Panel Plow, Screw Stop, Self-Regulating, without Handle	22.00
139	Boxwood or Rosewood Panel Plow, Screw Stop, Ivory-Tipped, Self-Regulating, without Handle	25.30
140	Boxwood or Rosewood Panel Plow, Screw Stop, Self-Regulating, with Handle	25.30
141	Boxwood or Rosewood Panel Plow, Screw Stop, Ivory-Tipped, Self-Regulating, with Handle	28.60
142	Ebony Panel Plow, Screw Stop, Self-Regulating, with Handle	38.50
143	Ebony Panel Plow, Screw Stop, Ivory-Tipped, Self-Regulating, with Handle	44.00
	Plow Bits, per set of Eight Irons	4.80

Plow Arms

	Price per Pair
Boxwood Plow Arms, Complete	$4.00
Boxwood Plow Arms, Ivory-Tipped, Complete	6.00
Rosewood Plow Arms, Complete	4.00
Rosewood Plow Arms, Ivory-Tipped, Complete	6.00
Applewood Plow Arms, Complete	3.00

Raising Planes

Stock No:		Size:	Price Each:
144	Raising Plane	2½″	$12.00
		2¾″	12.50
		3″	13.00
		3¼″	13.50
		3½″	14.00
		4″	14.50
145	Raising Plane, with Screw Arms	2½″	13.00
		2¾″	13.50
		3″	14.00
		3¼″	14.50
		3½″	15.00
		4″	15.50

Rabbet Planes

Nos. 146 and 150

Stock No.		Size	Price Each
146	Skew Rabbet Plane........	¼″ and ⅜″	$2.30
		½″, ¾″ and 1″	1.40
		1¼″	1.50
		1½″	1.60
		1¾″	1.90
		2″	2.00

For Rabbet Plane with One Cutter, add 40 cents; with Two Cutters, add 80 cents.

Stock No.		Size	Price Each
147	Skew Rabbet Plane, Boxed, With One Cutter........	$\frac{1}{2}$", $\frac{3}{4}$" and 1"	$2.40
		$1\frac{1}{4}$"	2.50
		$1\frac{1}{2}$"	2.60
		$1\frac{3}{4}$"	2.80
		2"	3.00

Stock No.		Size	Price Each
149	Buck Rabbet Plane, Skew, With Center Handle and Two Cutters............	1", $1\frac{1}{4}$", $1\frac{1}{2}$", $1\frac{3}{4}$" and 2"	$3.80
		$2\frac{1}{4}$" and $2\frac{1}{2}$"	4.50

Stock No.		Size	Price Each
$149\frac{1}{2}$	Buck Rabbet Plane, Skew, with Side Handle and Two Cutters............	1", $1\frac{1}{4}$", $1\frac{1}{2}$", $1\frac{3}{4}$" and 2"	$4.20
		$2\frac{1}{4}$" and $2\frac{1}{2}$"	4.90

Stock No.

150   Square Rabbet Plane—Same sizes and prices as No. 146 Skew Rabbet Plane.

Stock No.		Size	Price Each
151	Square Rabbet Plane, Boxed Face..................	$\frac{1}{2}$", $\frac{3}{4}$" and 1"	$2.40
		$1\frac{1}{4}$"	2.50
		$1\frac{1}{2}$"	2.60

Stock No.		Price per Pair
$151\frac{1}{2}$	Side Rabbet Planes, Right and Left...............	$5.00

Reeding Planes

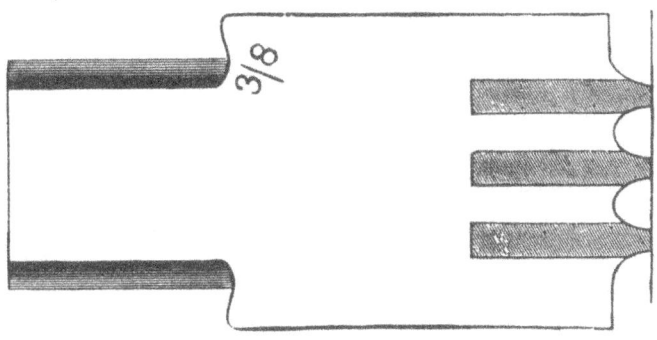

Stock No:		Size:	Price Each:
152	Reeding Plane, to make 1 Bead	¼″, ⅜″, and ½″	$3.00
	Reeding Plane, to make 2 Beads	¼″, ⅜″, and ½″	4.50
	Reeding Plane, to make 3 Beads	¼″, ⅜″, and ½″	6.00
	Reeding Plane, to make 4 Beads	¼″, ⅜″, and ½″	7.50
	Reeding Plane, to make 5 Beads	¼″, ⅜″, and ½″	8.00

For Reeding Planes above ½″, add 50 cents each.

Sash Planes

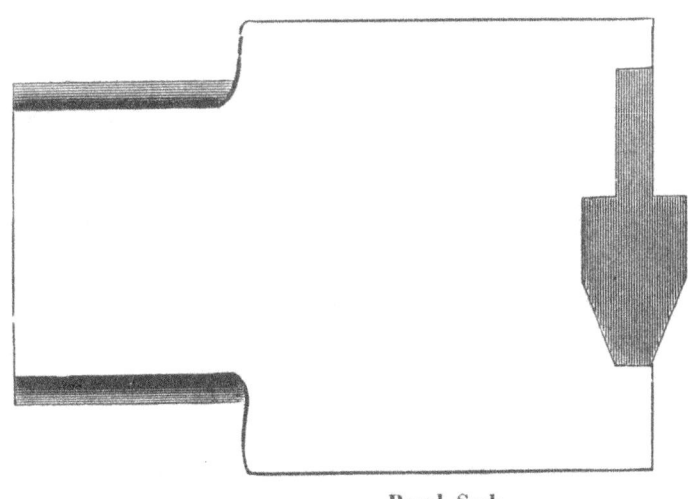

Bevel Sash

Sash Planes (Continued)

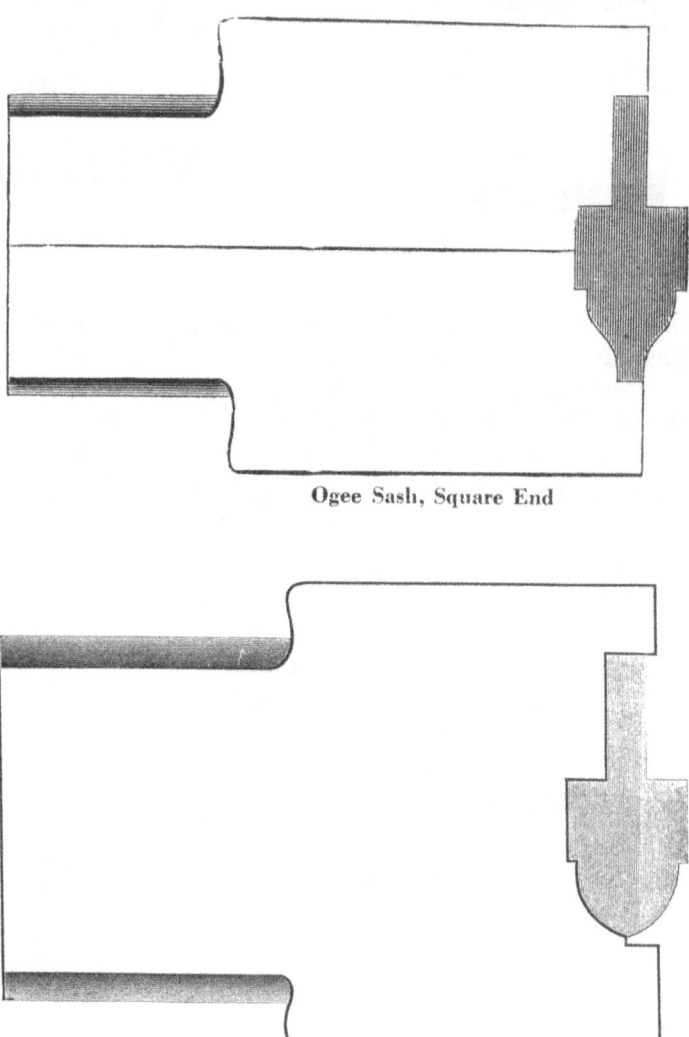

Ogee Sash, Square End

Gothic Sash

Sash Planes (Continued)

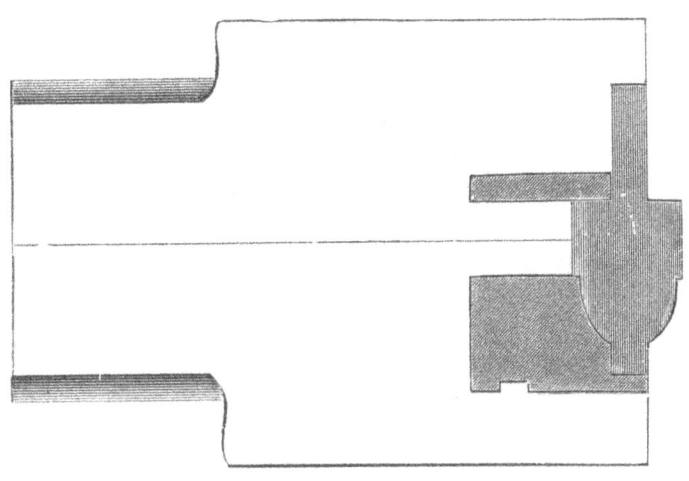

Ovolo Sash

Stock No:		Price Each:
155	Bevel or Ovolo Sash Plane, with One Iron	$2.40
156	Bevel or Ovolo Sash Plane, with Two Irons	3.00
157	Bevel or Ovolo Sash Plane, boxed, with Two Irons	3.60
164	Bevel or Ovolo Sash Plane, Self-Regulating, with Screw Arms	5.20
165	Gothic or Ogee Sash Plane, Self-Regulating, with Screw Arms	5.20
166	Bevel or Ovolo Sash Plane, boxed, Self-Regulating, with Screw Arms	6.00
167	Gothic or Ogee Sash Plane, boxed, Self-Regulating, with Screw Arms	6.00
168	Bevel or Ovolo Sash Planes, boxed, Dovetail, Self-Regulating, with Screw Arms	6.60
169	Gothic or Ogee Sash Planes, boxed, Dovetailed, Self-Regulating, with Screw Arms	6.60

Table Planes

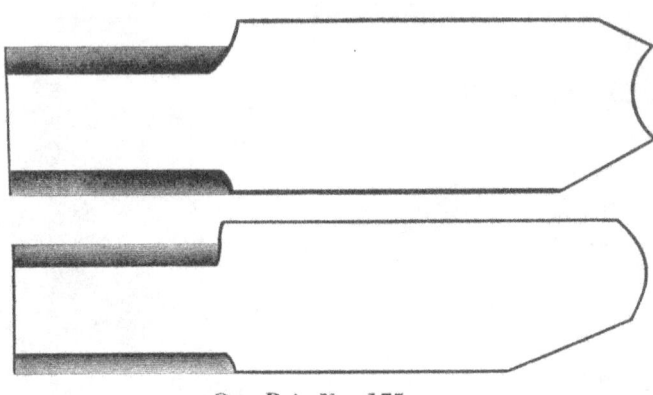

One Pair No. 175

Stock No:		Size:	Price Per Pair
175	Table Planes, with Gauge	½″ and ⅝″	$4.00
		¾″	5.00

176	Table Planes, with Gauge, boxed, Dovetailed		
		½″ and ⅝″	6.00
		¾″	7.00

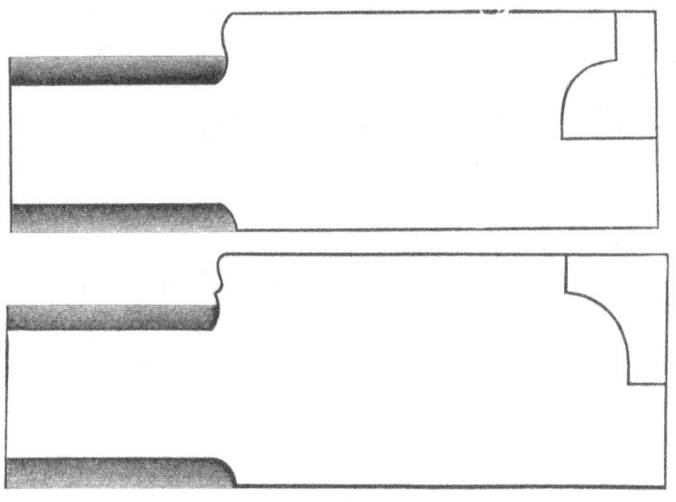

One Pair No. 177

177	Table Planes, with Fence	½″ and ⅝″	5.00
		¾″	6.00

Weather-Strip Planes

We supply all of the leading weather-strip manufacturers with special planes for installing their weather-strips. We manufacture a great many styles of these planes, and are in a position to make special planes to order at very reasonable prices.

The following planes can be used for installing most styles of weather-strips now on the market. We do not, however represent them to be suitable for every type, and urge our customers to send us samples of the weatherstrips to be installed if there is any doubt as to the kind of plane required.

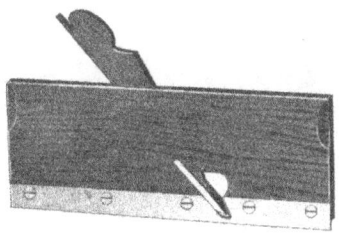 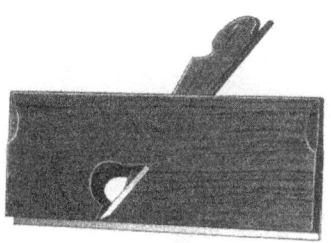

Stock No:	Size:	Price Each:
182 Special Rabbet or Meeting-Rail Plane, ½″ to 13/16″, by 16ths		$2.50

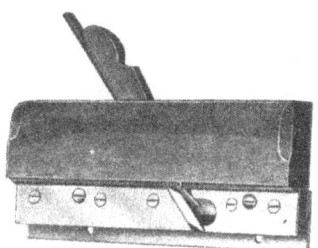 

Stock No:	Size:	Price Each:
183 Special Grooving Plane, with Adjustable Metal Fence, 7/64″ to ¼″, by 64ths		$4.00
184 Special Grooving Plane, with Adjustable Metal Fence, and Solid Handle, 7/64″ to ¼″, by 64ths		$5.00

Extra Special Grooving Bits for Nos. 183 and 184, $7.20 per doz.

Coopers' Wood Tools

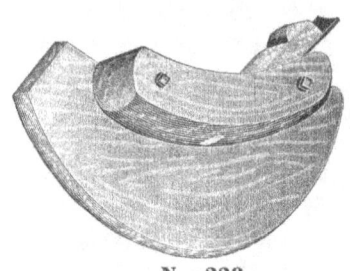
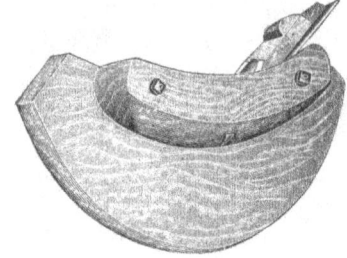

No. 228   No. 230

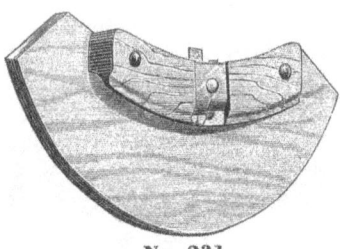
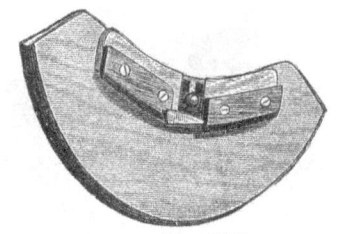

No. 231   No. 237

Stock No:		Price Each:
228	Stock Howel, all sizes, for Tight Work, 2″ Iron	$4.50
229	Beer Howel, all sizes, 2½″ Iron (Milwaukee Pattern)	7.50
230	Gouge Howel, all sizes, 1½″ Iron	5.50
231	Lance Croze, all sizes, for Tight Work	3.50
232	Champfer Tools, all sizes, for Tight Work	4.80
233	Lance Croze, all sizes, for Beer Kegs (Milwaukee Pat.)	7.50
234	Atchison Pattern Lignum—Vitae Croze, without Board	7.00
234A	Atchison Pattern Lignum—Vitae Croze, with Board	8.00
235	Shifting Croze, any size	4.50
235A	Post Shifting Croze, any size	4.50
236	Lignum—Vitae Howel Block, with Irons, ½″ to 1″	5.50
236A	Lignum—Vitae Croze Block, with Irons, any size	3.00
237	V-Croze, all sizes, Applewood Face, Maple Board	3.00
238	V-Croze, all sizes, Lignum—Vitae Face, Maple Board	1.80
238B	V-Croze, all sizes, Solid Applewood	4.50
238C	V-Croze, all sizes, Solid Lignum—Vitae	6.50
	Applewood Croze Boards	1.50
	Beech or Maple Croze Boards	1.00
	Lignum-Vitae Croze Boards	3.00

Coopers' Levelers

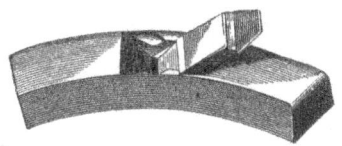

Stock No:		Price Each:
239	Solid Lignum-Vitae Coopers' Leveler	7.60
240	Applewood Coopers' Leveler	3.80
241	Beech Coopers' Leveler	3.00

Coopers' Applewood Tools

241A	Stock Howel, all sizes, for Tight Work, 2″ Iron	5.00
241B	Gouge Howel, all sizes, 1½″ Iron	6.00
241C	Lance Croze, all sizes, for Tight Work	4.00
241D	Lance Croze, all sizes, for Buckets	5.50
241E	Champfer Tools, all sizes, for Tight Work	5.50
241F	Beer Howel, 2½″ Iron, (Milwaukee Pattern)	9.00
241G	Beer Croze (Milwaukee Pattern)	9.00

Coopers' Floats

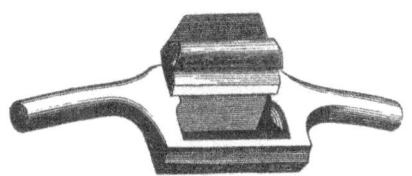

241K	Beech Float, Applewood Face	10.00
241L	Beech Float, Lignum—Vitae Face	10.50

Coopers' Drivers

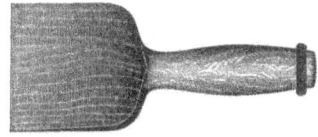

Stock No.		Price per Doz:
255	Coopers' Drivers, without Rings	$10.80
255½	Coopers' Drivers, with Rings	12.00

Bung Starters

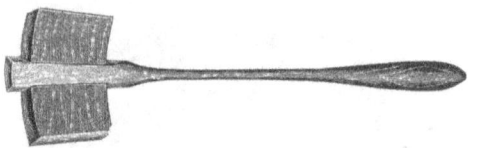

Stock No.		Price per Doz:
256	Maple Bung Starter, with Dovetailed Head	$12.00
257	Applewood Bung Starter, with Dovetailed Head	14.40
258	Lignum—Vitae Bung Starter, with Dovetailed Head	16.80

Coopers' Jointers

When ordering Coopers' Jointers, specify whether *Stave* or *Heading* Jointers are wanted.

Stock No:		Price Each:
242	Beech or Maple Jointer, 3 to 3½ ft. long, 2½" Single Iron	$10.00
244	Beech or Maple Jointer, 4 to 4½ ft. long, 2⅝" Single Iron	13.50
246	Beech or Maple Jointer, 5 to 5½ ft. long, 2¾" Single Iron	17.00
248	Beech or Maple Jointer, 6 ft. long, 2¾" Single Iron	20.50
248½	Beech or Maple Jointer, 3 to 3½ ft. long, 2½" Double Iron	$10.50
250	Beech or Maple Jointer, 4 to 4½ ft. long, 2⅝" Double Iron	14.00
252	Beech or Maple Jointer, 5 to 5½ ft. long, 2¾" Double Iron	17.50
254	Beech or Maple Jointer, 6 ft. long, 2¾" Double Iron	21.00

Applewood Coopers' Jointers

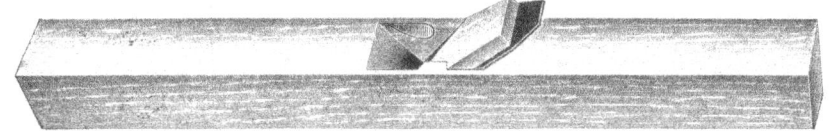

Stock No:			Price Each:
242	A	Applewood Jointer, 3 to 3½ ft. long, 2½" Single Iron	14.00
244	A	Applewood Jointer, 4 to 4½ ft. long, 2⅝" Single Iron	17.50
248½	A	Applewood Jointer, 3 to 3½ ft. long, 2½" Double Iron	14.50
250	A	Applewood Jointer, 4 to 4½ ft. long, 2⅝" Double Iron	18.00

Tank Builders' Jointers

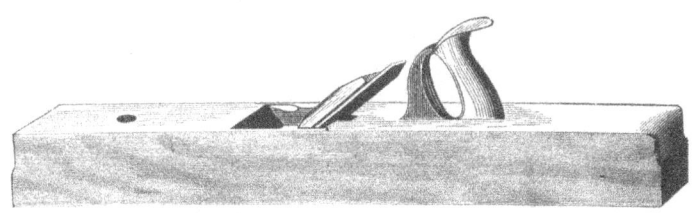

Tank Jointers
(All With 3-inch Double Irons)

Length:	Price Each:
22 Inches	$ 6.60
26 Inches	7.80
28 Inches	8.40
30 Inches	9.00
32 Inches	9.60
34 Inches	10.20
36 Inches	10.80
38 Inches	11.40
40 Inches	12.00

Extra 3" Double Irons for above	$2.00 Each
Extra 3" Single Irons for above	1.60 Each
Extra Handles for above	.60 Each
Tank Croze, Size 18"x1⅝"	7.00 Each

Mallets

Carpenters' Mallets

Stock No.		Price per Doz:
1	Round Hardwood Mallets, 5"x3"	$ 6.00
3	Round Hardwood Mallets, 5½"x3½"	7.20
5	Round Hardwood Mallets, 6"x4"	8.40
9	Round Lignum-Vitae Mallets, 5"x3"	9.60
11	Round Lignum-Vitae Mallets, 5½"x3½"	10.80
13	Round Lignum-Vitae Mallets, 6"x4"	12.00

Tinners' and Sheet Iron Mallets

Tinners' Mallet

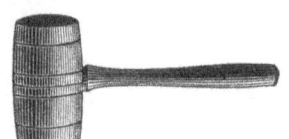

Sheet Iron Mallet

Stock No.		Price per Doz:
7	Round Hardwood Tinners' Mallets, 5½" long, assorted, 2" to 2½"	$4.80
7¼	Round Applewood Tinners' Mallets, 2" to 2½"	7.20
7½	Round Hardwood Sheet-Iron Mallets, 6"x2¾"	6.00
7¾	Round Applewood Sheet-Iron Mallets, 2¾"	8.40

Iron Ring Mallets

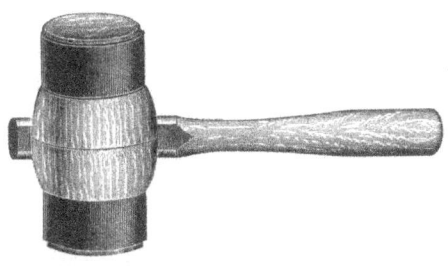

Stock No.		Price per Doz:
15	Round Hardwood Mallets, Mortised, with Iron Rings, 6"x4"	$17.40
17	Round Hardwood Mallets, Mortised, with Iron Rings 5½"x3½"	16.80

Square Mallets

Stock No.		Price per Doz:
2	Square Hardwood Mallets, 6"x2½"x3½"	$ 7.20
4	Square Hardwood Mallets, 6½"x2¾"x3¾"	8.40
6	Square Hardwood Mallets, 7"x3"x4"	9.60
8	Square Lignum-Vitae Mallets, 6"x2½"x3½"	10.80
10	Square Lignum-Vitae Mallets, 6½"x2¾"x3¾"	12.00
12	Square Lignum-Vitae Mallets, 7"x3"x4"	13.20

Marking Gauges

Stock No.:

185   Common Marking Gauge, Graduated in Inches ..... $2.40 per Doz.

Stock No.:

186   Panel Marking Gauge .... $6.00 per Dozen

Bench Plane Handles

Stock No.:

195   Beech Jack Plane Handles .... $1.92 per Dozen

Stock No:

197   Beech Fore Plane Handles .... $3.36 per Doz.

Saw Handles

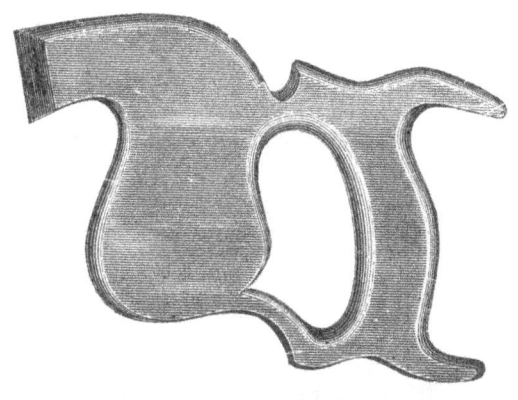

Stock No.		Price per Doz:
190	Cherry Saw Handles, full size, with Polished Edges	$5.76
191	Beech Saw Handles, full size, with Polished Edges	5.44
192	Beech Saw Handles, full size, with Plain Edges	5.12
193	Panel Saw Handles, with Polished Edges, for 16" and 20" Saws	3.04
194	Back Saw Handles, withPolished Edges	3.04

Chisel Handles

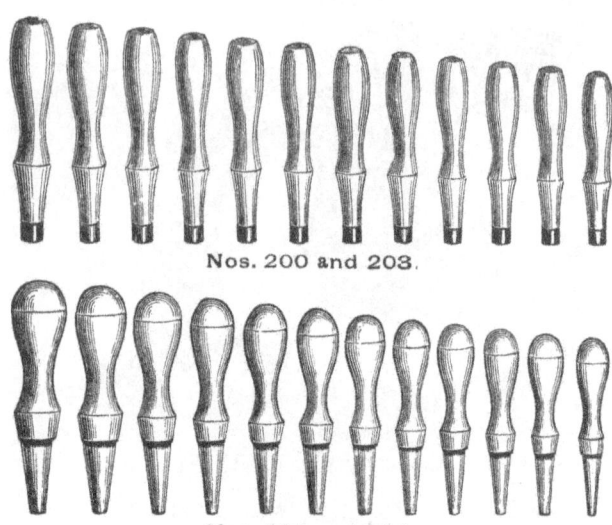

Nos. 200 and 203.

Nos. 201 and 204.

Plain Chisel Handles

Stock No.		Price per Gross
200	Plain Firmer Chisel Handles, assorted, 3 sizes in each box	$12.96
200½	Plain Firmer Chisel Handles, assorted, large, 3 sizes in each box	14.40
200¾	Plain Firmer Chisel Handles, assorted, extra large, 2 sizes in each box	17.28
201	Plain Socket Firmer Chisel Handles, assorted, 4 sizes in each box	11.52
201½	Plain Socket Firmer Chisel Handles, assorted, 3 sizes in each box	12.96

No. 202

202	Plain Socket Framing Chisel Handles, Iron Ferrules, assorted, 4 sizes in each box	14.40
202½	Plain Socket Framing Chisel Handles, Iron Ferrules, assorted, 2 sizes in each box	15.84
203	Plain Applewood Firmer Chisel Handles, assorted, 3 sizes in each box	14.40
203½	Plain Applewood Firmer Chisel Handles, assorted, large, 3 sizes in each box	17.28
203¾	Plain Applewood Firmer Chisel Handles, assorted, extra large, 2 sizes in each box	20.16
204	Plain Applewood Socket Firmer Chisel Handles, assorted 4 sizes in each box	12.96
204½	Plain Applewood Socket Firmer Chisel Handles, assorted, 3 sizes in each box	14.40

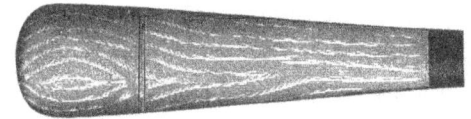

No. 205

205	Applewood Carver's Handles, assorted, 4 sizes in each box	18.72

Leather-Top Chisel Handles

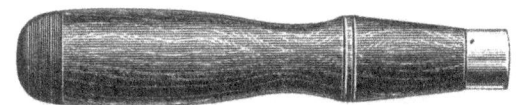

Nos. 200 and 200½

One dozen in a paper box.

Stock No.		Price per Gross
200 LT	Tanged Firmer, Leather-Top Chisel Handles, assorted, 3 sizes, Nos. 1, 2, and 3	$18.72
200½LT	Tanged Firmer, Leather-Top Chisel Handles, assorted, 3 sizes, Nos. 2, 3, and 4	20.16

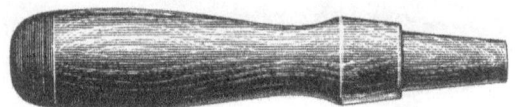

Nos. 201 and 201½
One dozen in a paper box.

201 LT   Socket Firmer, Leather-Top Chisel Handles,
assorted, 4 sizes, Nos. 0, 1, 2, and 3 .... 17.28
201½LT   Socket Firmer, Leather-Top Chisel Handles,
assorted, 3 sizes, Nos. 2, 3, and 4 .... 18.72

Nos. 202 and 202½
One dozen in a paper box.

202 LT   Socket Framing, Leather-Top Chisel Handles,
assorted, 4 sizes, Nos. 0, 1, 2, and 3 .... 20.16
202½LT   Socket Framing, Leather-Top Chisel Handles,
assorted, 2 sizes, Nos. 2 and 3 .... 21.60

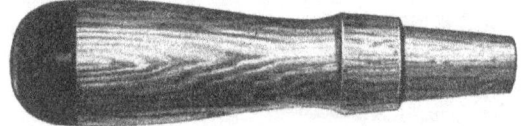

Butt Socket Firmer
One dozen in a paper box.

Butt Socket Firmer, Leather-Top Chisel Handles
assorted, 4 sizes, Nos. 0, 1, 2, and 3 .... 20.16

Softwood File Handles

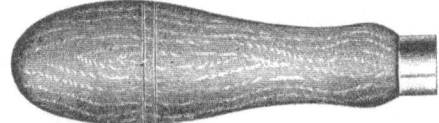

No. 212

Stock No.   Price per Gross
212   File Handles, with Brass Ferrules, assorted, 3 sizes,
4 dozen in each box $5.76
213   File Handles, with Brass Ferrules, assorted, large,
2 sizes, 3 dozen in each box 8.64

Hardwood Auger Handles

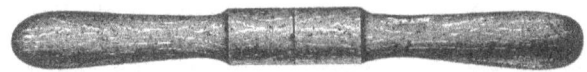

No. 216A

Stock No.   Price per Gross
216A   Auger Handles, assorted, 3 sizes, Nos. 1, 2, and 3 .... $28.80

www.ingramcontent.com/pod-product-compliance
Lightning Source LLC
LaVergne TN
LVHW092228200326
834410LV00020B/121